LEAVE THE CAVE

BECOMING A MAN OF GREAT EXPLOITS, MOVING FROM PASSIVITY TO PURPOSE

NEIL KENNEDY

Contents

1

Manhood in Crisis

I cry out to God Most High, to God who fulfills His purpose for me. – Psalm 57:2

Manhood in crisis.

We're in deep trouble. I know.

For over a decade, I have devoted my life and all my efforts to communicating with men — encouraging, engaging, and empowering them to resurrect Biblical/Authentic manhood. I can tell you that we're facing unprecedented challenges. If I were to go statistical, you would become bored and skip over the data. If I were to create a laundry list of negatives, you would exhale with disgust and shrink back. Rather than that, let's get to the point.

You have an enemy. Your enemy hates you. I refer to your enemy as an anti-man spirit. He is a master manipulator. His art is mendacity. He is the father of lies. He will use all of his tricks, schemes, and devices to entrap you. His entire objective is to destroy mankind; to do so, he must first redefine manhood.

The anti-man spirit is powerless against a man of God. You threaten his end-game. If you understand your purposes, pursue God's original intent for Biblical/Authentic manhood, and walk in the directional intent of discipleship, you're unstoppable.

You're a man.

Your desire to step up to Biblical/Authentic manhood is evident. You wouldn't be holding this book without the commitment to authenticity. To be counter-cultural is not for the faint of heart. It takes courage to be manly in today's climate of misandry — a deep contempt, bias, and hatred of men.

Manhood is facing an identity crisis. Our nemesis — the agent of our downfall — is redefining masculinity by moving the biological boundary stones of gender identities.

It is hard to comprehend that even medical professionals are willingly surrendering their credibility to propagate the lie that a man can be a woman and a woman can be a man. This mendacious narrative has confused the average young man about his manhood, masculinity, and sexuality.

> If you don't know WHO you are, you will never WHY you are.

Inherent to identity is purpose.

I hope that by the end of this book, you have an unwavering assurance of your manhood. You'll need it.

If you're going to do anything significant for God, you will face intimidating fears, waves of doubt, clouds of depression, and suggestions of failure. You will experience slander, false accusations, betrayals, and lies. Family members and friends may mock you. Co-workers may scoff at you. Social platforms may block you. You will engage in a spiritual warfare like none other.

However, greater is He that is within you than he that is in the world.

I don't want to assume that you've read my story in the other books that I've written. Let me briefly make you aware of where I am coming from and why this is an important message for me to tell men.

My father exited my life when I was five years of age. My mother left him for her lover on Christmas day. Her betrayal broke his heart. Rather than fight to keep my siblings and me in his life, he abandoned the effort and devoted his life to his new wife and her five children.

My father's voice became muted. He would not be there to tell me about my heritage, nor would he be there to prophesy my future. Fatherlessness is a deep wound.

Shortly after, my mother and her new husband sat me down and informed me that I would no longer be called by my birth name, Gary Neil Kennedy. I would be called Neil and assume her husband's name, Roberson. I wasn't adopted. The new name was assumed on me, which created confusion and an identity crisis in my life.

Growing up, I never knew who I was. If you don't know who you are, you will never understand why you are.

My entire childhood and teenage years were marked with confusion. My father-wound festered for years.

> When the purpose is unknown, abuse is inevitable.
> — Dr. Myles Munroe

A purpose is the why of manhood.

Deep within the heart of a man are purposes. If you have read FIVESTARMAN, you know the five passions of Biblical/Authentic manhood. If not, go to FIVESTARMAN.COM, and I will deliver you a free copy. Let me say a few things about the why of manhood to lay the foundation for where we're going with this book.

> *The purpose in a man's heart is like deep water, but a man of understanding will draw it out.* — *Proverbs 20:5 ESV*

Many translations have neutered the word for man in this verse. There are three Hebrew words for man:

- **âdam** - human, mankind, human race, sometimes used as a genitive after adjectives.
- **ěnôwsh** - mortal man, person, mankind, men (collective)
- **îysh** - man, male, husband, servant, champion, great man, citizen, warrior, manly-minded, valiant, priest, intelligent, noble quality.

Proverbs 20:5 uses îysh, which means masculine male as opposed to a female. As noted above, îysh is a rich and descriptive word identifying manhood. I've categorized the purposes of man into five passions that empower a man in the pursuit of

Biblical/Authentic manhood:

1. Adventure
2. Entrepreneur
3. Gallant
4. Faithful
5. Philanthropic

When a man understands these five passions of his purpose, his life takes on meaning and motivation like no other. I have seen men move from passivity to purpose when these passions are stirred up.

> *For this reason, I remind you to fan into flame the gift of God, which is in you through the laying on of my hands.*
> *— 2 Timothy 1:6*

Paul reminds his protege to stoke the embers of what was burning inside him. He says that we are saved and called to a holy life—not because of anything we have done but because of His purpose and grace (verse 9). We're called to a religious life. That is not exclusive to mean that we are pure, but it also means that we are set apart for His purpose.

Your purpose arouses violent opposition.

As I mentioned earlier, because you're a man in an anti-man culture, you're facing a malevolent enemy. I can't stress enough the antipathy that he has against you. You won't be able to appease him. You can't negotiate. You can't ignore him. Unless you surrender your manhood to his totalitarian governance over your life, he will fight you tooth and nail — using all of his resources to wholly and utterly destroy you.

> You will never win the battle that you're unwilling to confront.

You were born in a time of war.

Over the last decade, in my interactions with hundreds of thousands of men, I have concluded that most men are not engaged in the fight. They are retreating or even surrendering. It is sad. It's cowardly.

> Every man will face a time in his life to either step up and be a man or shrink back into obscurity.

I believe it is a cowardly generation that will not fight the foe that desires to dominate men, rape women, molest girls, and enslave boys. It's evil.

C.S. Lewis describes this evil in Mere Christianity — *"One of the things that surprised me when I first read the New Testament seriously was that it talked so much about a Dark Power in the universe—a mighty evil spirit who was held to be the Power behind death, disease, and sin. The difference is that Christianity thinks this Dark Power was created by God and was good when he was created until he went wrong. Christianity agrees...this universe is at war."*

The evil is not just the enemy. It is the passivity of men.

Passivity paralyzes men.

Passivity is the state of being inactive or without standing against your opposition. Don't misread what I am suggesting.

There is wisdom in avoiding conflict. Not every battle is worthy of your high calling. However, when it comes to protecting Biblical/Authentic manhood, this is not something that we need to withdraw from.

Here are some ways in which passivity can paralyze men:

- **Passivity can lead to a lack of motivation and ambition.** When men are passive, they are less likely to set goals for themselves and take action to achieve them. This can lead to a feeling of stagnation and dissatisfaction in life.
- **Passivity can make it difficult to make decisions.** When men are passive, they are more likely to avoid making decisions altogether. This can lead to missed opportunities and regret later on.
- **Passivity can cause a man to be double-minded.** Duplicity is deadly. It causes a man to be unstable in all that he does. He is unreliable. His family never knows where he stands on issues or values.
- **Passivity can make it difficult to stand up for oneself and others.** When men are passive, they are less likely to speak up when they see something wrong or to defend themselves or others. This can lead to feelings of helplessness and victimization.
- **Passivity can make it difficult to form and maintain healthy relationships.** When men are passive, they are less likely to put in the effort required to build and maintain strong relationships. This can lead to loneliness and isolation.
- **Passive men typically remain single.** They are not proactive in building a relationship with a woman. If they do marry,

they are usually weak leaders. Passive husbands become boys in the relationship, and the wives become mothers to them.

Overall, passivity can have a number of negative consequences for men. It can lead to a lack of motivation, ambition, and decision-making skills. It can also make it difficult to stand up for oneself and others and to form and maintain healthy relationships.

Perhaps the Lord is with you!

The Israelites were weaponless in battling their enemies. Only King Saul and Jonathan had weapons. Jonathan convinces his armor barrier to sneak over to the Philistine outpost without telling his father. As they arrive at the cliff with the army above them, Jonathan says, *"Perhaps the Lord will act on our behalf. Nothing can hinder the Lord from saving, whether by many or by few."* (1 Samuel 14:6)

Jonathan provokes the Philistines to invite an attack. Jonathan climbed up the cliff with his armor-bearer right behind him. Jonathan killed twenty men in the fight. The Philistines panic in confusion and begin to strike one another.

> *When all the Israelites who had hidden in the hill country*
> *of Ephraim heard that the Philistines were on the run,*
> *they joined the battle in hot pursuit. — 1 Samuel 14:22*

Because Jonathan said, *"Perhaps the Lord is with us,"* and engaged in the fight, those paralyzed by passivity were stirred up and joined the battle. The Israelites pursued the enemy because Jonathan was unwilling to surrender to their enemy's domination.

Perhaps the Lord is with us!

Rather than sit still in our strongholds — modern-day man caves — perhaps the Lord will empower us to overcome our challenges.

If you are a man who is struggling with passivity, there are several things you can do to overcome it:

- **Set goals for yourself and take action to achieve them.** Even if you don't know exactly what you want to do with your life, start by setting small goals for yourself and working towards them. This will help you to develop a sense of motivation and ambition.
- **Challenge yourself to make decisions, even small ones.** When you are faced with a decision, take a few minutes to think about your options and make the best decision you can. Even if you make the wrong decision, you will learn from your mistake and become better at making decisions in the future.
- **Stand up for yourself and others, even when it's difficult.** If you see something wrong, speak up. If someone is being mistreated, defend them. It may not be easy, but it's essential to stand up for what you believe in.
- **Put in the effort to build and maintain strong relationships.** Be there for your friends and family when they need you. Make time for them, even when you're busy. And be willing to compromise and communicate effectively.

Overcoming passivity takes time and effort, but it is possible. By following these tips, you can become more assertive and take control of your life.

A man stands up.

> *Defend the poor and fatherless;*
>   *Do justice to the afflicted and needy. — Psalm 82:3*

My wife and I were standing in a line at a theme park when a young, arrogant man spoke harshly, even physically threatening a young boy behind him. The boy got too close to the young man. The boy withdrew behind his mother. I could see the fear in the boy. Without hesitation, in a calm yet authoritative manner, I stepped forward and addressed the young man, "Don't speak to that boy in that way."

"Who are you?" the young man scoffed.

"I am a man that will defend this boy," I replied.

"You're an old man!" he snuffed.

"Maybe, but I am also experienced. I can take you in seconds. Not minutes. Not hours. In seconds, you will be whimpering for mercy," I assured him.

Jesus is not nice.

Some men reading this book will piously say, "What would Jesus do?"

I can assure you that Jesus is kind, yet He is not passive, nor is He nice.

The word nice comes from the Latin *nescius,* "ignorant," and *nescire*, "not know." Other senses include "coy, reserved, passive, timid, diminutive, or play small."

You can't reduce Jesus to be the Savior you're comfortable with—you must accept Who He is.

Many people only think of Jesus as the whipped, beaten, dominated, crucified man on the cross. In reality, Jesus is presently the resurrected, glorified, and enthroned King of kings and Lord of lords.

Jesus is a Warrior, and when He returns, He certainly won't be nice.

The Bible is clear, *"The Fear of the Lord*—that is wisdom; when you understand the times, you will forsake (stand against) Evil." (Read Job 28:28)

Our culture has no fear of the Lord.

The Apostle Paul warned Timothy that there would be terrible times in the last days. People will be lovers of themselves, lovers of money, boastful, proud, abusive, disobedient to their parents, ungrateful, unholy, without love, unforgiving, slanderous, without self-control, brutal, not lovers of the good, treacherous, rash, conceited, lovers of pleasure rather than lovers of God.

When you play nice:

- You won't have the courage to confront Evil.
- You tolerate what you should rebuke.
- You're dominated by what you should defeat.
- You're passive-aggressive when you should take action.
- Your stomach becomes your god (Philippians 3:19).
- You're held captive by invisible chains.

We are kind to people, but not nice with Evil.

Be angry [at sin—at immorality, at injustice, at ungodly behavior], yet do not sin; do not let your anger [cause you shame, nor allow it to] last until the sun goes down. And do not give the devil an opportunity [to lead you into sin by holding a grudge, or nurturing anger, or harboring resentment, or cultivating bitterness]. — Ephesians 4:26-27

As men, we must be careful not to allow the Devil to manipulate our anger. Manipulation is a type of witchcraft. The enemy will use this tactic for you to harbor anger until you explode unwisely. We must distinguish the different types of anger and extinguish the harmful emotions.

- **RAGE** is a wave of anger that causes us to flurry about with over-expressed gestures, clinched jaws, or boisterous words, even calling down curses.
- **FURY** is a much stronger emotion of rage. It is a destructive form of rage, often leading to a depraved mind and delusional violence.
- **INDIGNATION** is righteous anger caused by witnessing or experiencing injustice, shame, or evil done to innocence. It is what moves us to risk our lives to protect others.
- **WRATH** is the godliest form of anger. It is an anger that responds to evil with pure judgment. Wrath cleanses the Earth of evil.

Here are some tips for extinguishing harmful emotions:

- **Identify the triggers.** What are the things that typically make you angry? Once you know your triggers, you can start to develop strategies for avoiding them or coping with them in a healthy way.
- **Take a break.** If you feel yourself getting angry, take a few minutes to calm down before you say or do anything you

might regret. Go for a walk, listen to music, or take a deep breath.

- **Pray.** Ask the Holy Spirit to help you with His fruit— love, joy, peace, patience, kindness, goodness, faithfulness, gentleness, and self-control.
- **Express your anger in a healthy way.** Once you have calmed down, you can express your anger in a healthy way, such as by talking to a trusted friend or family member, writing in a journal, or exercising.

Here are some tips for using indignation and wrath wisely:

- **Make sure that your anger is justified.** Before you act on your anger, make sure that you are truly responding to injustice or evil.
- **Be proportional in your response.** Your response to injustice or evil should be reasonable and proportionate.
- **Seek to bring about justice and righteousness.** Your goal should be to bring about a positive outcome, not to simply punish the wrongdoer.

By distinguishing the different types of anger and extinguishing the harmful emotions, we can live more peaceful and productive lives.

Manhood has a presence.

When a man walks into the room, people take notice. There is an awe to Biblical/Authentic manhood. It isn't boastful. It isn't rude. It isn't demanding. It is a quiet demeanor of presence.

Like the old Spaghetti Westerns that Clint Eastwood made— when he would walk into the bar and suddenly the music stops, heads turn, and wicked men squirmed. His presence spoke louder than his whispered words. The message was clear, "You don't want to tangle with me."

I am not talking about being a "tough guy" grunting out meathead threats. Please hear me. I am talking about having a presence of godly authority in your life.

Authentic manhood has a presence. It is a presence that is felt by others, even if they cannot articulate it. It is a presence that is rooted in confidence, integrity, and compassion.

Men who have an authentic presence are not afraid to be themselves. They are comfortable in their own skin, and they know who they are. They are also men of their word. They keep their promises, and they are always there for the people who matter to them.

Men with an authentic presence are also compassionate. They care about others, and they want to make a difference in the world. They are not afraid to stand up for what is right, even when it is difficult.

Here are some of the characteristics of authentic manhood presence:

- **Confidence:** Authentic men are confident in themselves and their abilities. They are not arrogant or boastful, but they carry themselves with an air of assurance that comes with knowing who they are in Christ Jesus.
- **Integrity:** Authentic men are honest and trustworthy. They keep their promises, and they do what they say they are going to do. They watch over their words.
- **Compassion:** Authentic men are compassionate and caring. They have empathy for others, and they are always willing

to help those in need. When Jesus saw the helpless and harassed, He was moved with compassion.

- **Strength:** Authentic men are strong, both physically and mentally. They are able to overcome challenges, and they are always there for the people they love. We draw our strength from God, then we turn and strengthen our families.
- **Humility:** Authentic men are humble. They are not afraid to admit their mistakes, and they are always willing to learn wisdom from others. Learning is not a weakness. Everyone has a right to grow.

Authentic manhood presence is not something that can be faked. It comes from a deep understanding of yourself and your values. It also comes from living a life that aligns with those values.

If you want to develop an authentic manhood presence, the first step is to get to know yourself. What are your values? What are your strengths and weaknesses? What are your goals and dreams? Once you have a better understanding of yourself, you can start to live a life that aligns with those values.

Can you define your specific purposes? Remember, if you do not know your purpose, your life will be filled with abuse. You'll abuse people, substances, and money.

Living an authentic life is not always easy, but it is always worth it. When you live an authentic life, you will develop a strong presence that will attract others to you. You will also be more likely to achieve your goals and live a fulfilling life.

2

The Heart of Manhood

Behold, you delight in truth in the inward being, and you teach me wisdom in the secret heart. — *Psalm 51:6*

What you fail to destroy will eventually destroy you.

The first King of Israel, Saul, was disqualified from the office. He disobeyed the Word of the Lord. He was clearly instructed to eradicate the Amalekites. That meant that nothing was to survive. Yet, Saul kept the best of the spoils and allowed the elites to remain alive.

Leaving the wicked Agag of the Amalekites alive will have lasting repercussions even today. An anti-Christ spirit will travel through the descendants of Agag. Hamon, one of those descendants, will take up the offense against Mordechai and attempt to annihilate the Jews. That same spirit will again raise its evil head against the Jews during the pogrom in Russia, wreaking havoc and violently attacking them. The perpetrators of pogroms, with the assistance and support of local police, raped and murdered Jewish women and men. Of course, that evil spirit enticed Adolf Hitler to launch Kristallnacht, a concerted effort for citizens to riot and attack Jews.

Now, in recent weeks, the spirit of Agag has arisen in Hamas, which is the Hebrew word for violence. This terrorist group subjugates the Palestinian people, hiding behind women and children to do their evil works against the Jews.

God has the foreknowledge of outcomes. When God gave King Saul the responsibility to utterly destroy Agag and the Amalekites, He was looking ahead to see the horrific destruction to innocent lives if they were to remain alive.

Saul failed to destroy Agag; therefore, Agag is working to destroy the Jewish people.

David is discovered in obscurity.

You remember the incredible story of David. It is one of the best narratives of a hero's journey.

David starts as a shepherd, minding his father's sheep, when a prophet shows up at his home. The Prophet Samuel is commissioned to anoint the heir-to-the-throne of Israel.

When Samuel arrives at the home of Jesse and announces his intent, the sons line up—oldest to youngest. Eliab stands tall and robust. His appearance is striking. He looks like a leader. So much so that even the fore-teller expects to be anointing him. The Spirit says, *"Do not consider him; I've rejected him. The Lord does not look at the things people look at. People look at the outward appearance, but the Lord looks at the heart."*

For as he thinks in his heart, so is he. — Proverbs 23:7

The Hebrew words for the heart are *lêb and nephesh*, which

indicate a man's inner man, mind, will, understanding, moral character, and soul. The heart is the seat of purposes, seat of appetites, seat of passions, and seat of courage.

In my book, *Bedding Ishtar*, I spend a few chapters on these seats of the heart. I recommend that you get a copy at Fivestar-Man.com.

Suffice it to say, Eliab was not the man. He is disqualified.

Abinadab is next. He is rejected.

Shammah is third. He is rejected.

Seven sons parade before the Prophet, but Samuel does not see a King in them.

Confused, Samuel asks, "Are these all the sons you have?"

"There is still the youngest," Jesse answered. "He is tending the sheep."

David is summoned from the pasture.

As soon as David arrives, the Spirit tells the Prophet, "Rise and anoint him; this is the one."

Samuel anointed David with oil, and the Spirit came on him powerfully.

What made the difference? What distinguished David from his brothers?

I believe it was David's preparation in isolation.

> Champions are prepared in secret; they are revealed
> in the contest.

As a shepherd, David spent a lot of time tending his father's sheep. Shepherding can be a lonely job. I've shared some of this before, but it is worth repeating.

Who you are in secret is who you become in public.

When you're alone, you can learn who you are and what you can become. Isolation can be detrimental for a confused man; however, it can be a place of training for someone preparing for a purpose.

Isolation taught me:

- **Isolation can be intimidating.** You are vulnerable. Your weaknesses are exposed. Your insecurities are revealed.
- **Isolation is quiet.** Suddenly, your internal ear is hearing more than your external ear.
- **Isolation is revealing.** A gift of discernment becomes enlightened in isolation.
- **Isolation can expand your beliefs.** Crowds can limit your space. Your shoulders drop. You become cramped. Isolation expands you. Crowds can confine you. Isolation can enlarge you.
- **Isolation tests your character.** Who you are in secret is what moves you in public.
- **Isolation prepares you.** Promotion comes from what you do when no one is watching you.

It was in the secret place of the field that David was prepared. David considered what he was doing important, while others deemed small tasks and insignificant adventures.

Slaves, obey your earthly masters with respect and fear, and with sincerity of heart, just as you would obey Christ. Obey them not only to win their favor when their eye is on you, but as slaves of Christ, doing the will of God from your heart. Serve wholeheartedly, as if you were serving the Lord, not people, because you know that the Lord will reward each one for whatever good they do, whether they are slave or free. — Ephesians 6:5-8

The secret to promotion is serving through a man, not to a man.

David wasn't just serving his earthly father. David was serving his Heavenly Father. While he was shepherding, he began to strum his guitar and sing prophetic songs. David considered shepherding a critical assignment. And that is why God discovered him.

Here are some examples of how shepherds fulfill these responsibilities:

- **Caring for the physical needs of the sheep:** Shepherds may use various methods to provide food and water for their sheep, such as grazing, hay feeding, and grain feeding. They may also use portable fencing to keep the sheep in areas with good forage and to protect them from predators.
- **Leading the sheep to a good pasture:** Shepherds use their knowledge of the local landscape and weather conditions to find the best pasture for their sheep. They may also use dogs to help them herd the sheep to new grazing areas.
- **Gathering the sheep together:** Shepherds may use various methods to gather their sheep, such as calling their names, using a whistle, or using a sheepdog.
- **Protecting the sheep from harm:** Shepherds may use various methods to protect them from predators, such as guard dogs, fences, and night grazing.

- **Healing the sick and injured sheep:** Shepherds may provide basic first aid to ill or injured sheep, such as cleaning and dressing wounds.

Amazingly, shepherding can be precisely what leading people is meant to be.

When God needs a leader, He looks for a servant.

I can't tell you how many men I've known assume leadership positions without preparing themselves for it. A novice leader is destructive.

> *One who is slack in his work is brother to one who destroys.*
> *— Proverbs 18:9*

When God wants a leader, He looks for a servant. The only Biblical-endorsed leadership is servant leadership. Jesus said that if you want to be great in the Kingdom, you must become a servant to all (Matthew 20:26). The world system of leadership is overbearing, which is, in fact, satanic.

> Any leadership that is designed to be served rather than to serve is satanic in nature. — Jeff Ables

The primary difference between servant leadership and authoritarian leadership is that servant leaders focus on serving others, while domineering leaders focus on controlling others.

Servant leaders are humble and put the needs of their team members first. Servant leaders believe their role is to empower their team members to succeed. They understand the protocol of authority places them under authority so that they can manage what they are placed over with authority. In other words, authority flows through leadership, not just from their leadership.

Domineering leaders, on the other hand, are focused on maintaining power and control. They are often demanding and micromanaging their team members. Autocratic leaders may also be bullies and use intimidation to get their way. They are often narcissistic with paranoia and suspicions.

Servant leadership is a more practical style of leadership than domineering leadership. Servant leaders are likelier to create a positive and productive work environment where team members feel valued and respected. This can lead to increased employee engagement, productivity, and satisfaction.

Domineering leadership, on the other hand, can lead to a harmful and toxic work environment. Team members may feel disengaged, demotivated, and stressed. This can decrease employee productivity and satisfaction and may also increase turnover rates.

If you are a leader, striving to be a servant leader is essential. Servant leadership is a more effective and sustainable way to lead in the long term.

> *But Jesus called them to him and said, "You know that the rulers of the Gentiles lord it over them, and their great ones exercise authority over them. It shall not be so among you. But whoever would be great among you must be your servant, and whoever would be first among you must be your slave, even as the Son of Man came not to be served but to serve and to give his life as a ransom for many." — Matthew 20:25–28*

Unfortunately, I have known leaders of large businesses, organizations, and churches who lead with intimidation and domination rather than as Christ encouraged us to be servants.

Our example of Biblical leadership is God, Jehovah-Rohi, the Lord is our Shepherd.

> *Psalm 23:1 (ESV)*
> *The Lord is my shepherd, I lack nothing.*
> *He makes me lie down in green pastures,*
> *he leads me beside quiet waters,*
> *he refreshes my soul.*
> *He guides me along the right paths*
> *for his name's sake.*
> *Even though I walk*
> *through the darkest valley,*
> *I will fear no evil,*
> *for you are with me;*
> *your rod and your staff,*
> *they comfort me.*
> *You prepare a table before me*
> *in the presence of my enemies.*
> *You anoint my head with oil;*
> *my cup overflows.*
> *Surely, your goodness and love will follow me*
> *all the days of my life,*
> *and I will dwell in the house of the Lord*
> *forever.*

Jehovah Rohi is our Good Shepherd. He loves us, cares for us,

protects us, and provides for all of our needs. We can trust Him to lead us through life and to bring us to our eternal home in heaven.

Biblical Benefits of the Name Jehovah Rohi (The LORD Our Shepherd) Jehovah Rohi provides for our needs.

- He feeds us with spiritual food (Psalm 23:1).
- He leads us to fresh pastures and still waters (Psalm 23:2).
- He provides all that we need physically and spiritually (Psalm 23:1).

Jehovah Rohi protects us.

- He is with us even in the darkest valleys (Psalm 23:4).
- He protects us from our enemies (Psalm 23:5).
- He gives us peace and security (Psalm 23:4).

Jehovah Rohi cares for us.

- He knows our needs and desires (Psalm 23:2).
- He restores our souls (Psalm 23:3).
- He guides us on the right path (Psalm 23:3).

Jehovah Rohi loves us.

- He laid down His life for us (John 10:11).
- He calls us His sheep (John 10:27).
- He promises never to leave us or forsake us (Hebrews 13:5).

Additional Biblical Benefits of Jehovah Rohi

- He seeks and saves the lost (Luke 19:10).
- He forgives our sins (Psalm 23:3).
- He heals our broken hearts (Psalm 23:3).
- He gives us eternal life (John 10:28).

We need to model our leadership as David recognized the leadership of Jehovah-Rohi, his Good Shepherd.

David was a shepherd. So, when God needed a shepherd for His people, He looked at the fields of Israel and found David in obscurity. Then, God sent the Prophet Samuel to anoint the Shepherd of Israel.

You may be thinking that you're wasting your time. You may consider that you're living in obscurity and that God doesn't even know your address. But I want to assure you that God knows how and when to reach you.

> When God wants leaders, He looks for servants.
> *Slaves, obey your earthly masters with deep respect and fear. Serve them sincerely as you would serve Christ. Try to please them all the time, not just when they are watching you. As slaves of Christ, do the will of God with all your heart. Work with enthusiasm, as though you were working for the Lord rather than for people. Remember that the Lord will reward each one of us for the good we do, whether we are slaves or free. - Ephesians 6:5-8 (NLT)*

Biblical leaders serve the LORD.

The key to servant leadership is to serve *through* a man rather than *to* a man. We're not just serving a man. We're serving

Christ. When we approach our work this way, we rely on promotion from our LORD.

> *Humble yourselves before the Lord, and he will exalt you.*
> *- James 4:10*

The word exalt in Greek is *hypsoō*, which means to rise to dignity, honor, happiness, to the very summit of opulence and prosperity.

It seems paradoxical, but humility is the stepping stone to promotion in the Kingdom of God.

Here are 5 Biblical steps to promotion from the Lord:

1. **Seek first the Kingdom of God and His righteousness, and all these things shall be given to you as well.** (Matthew 6:33). This means that our primary focus should be serving God and doing His will, rather than our ambitions. When we put God first, He will care for us and provide for our needs, including promotion.

2. **Be faithful in the little things.** (Luke 16:10) God is looking for people who are faithful in the small things because He knows that if we are faithful in the small things, we will also be faithful in the big things. God will promote us to greater responsibility when we are faithful in our current positions.

3. **Be humble and teachable.** (Proverbs 11:2) God promotes the humble but resists the proud. When we are humble, we are willing to learn and grow. We are also more likely to listen to others and to receive feedback. God wants to promote people who are teachable and willing to learn from

their mistakes.

4. **Be a good steward of what God has given you.** (Matthew 25:21) God is looking for people who are good stewards of what He has given them. This means we are faithful to manage our resources, time, and talents wisely. When we are good stewards, God can trust us with greater responsibility.

5. **Be patient and trust God's timing.** (Psalm 27:14) God's timing is not always our timing. He may have us wait for promotion for a reason. He may be preparing us for a more significant role or teaching us something important. When we are patient and trust God's timing, He will promote us at the right time.

Here are some additional Bible verses that support these steps:

- **Proverbs 22:29** – "Do you see a man skilled in his work? He will stand before kings; he will not stand before unknown men."
- **1 Timothy 4:12** – "Don't let anyone look down on you because you are young, but set an example for the believers in speech, conduct, love, faith, and purity."
- **Titus 3:14** – "Our people must learn to devote themselves to doing good works to meet urgent needs, so that they may not be unfruitful."
- **James 4:10** – "Humble yourselves before the Lord, and He will exalt you."
- **Ecclesiastes 3:11** – "He has made everything beautiful in its time. He has put eternity in their hearts, but no one can discover what God has done from the beginning to the end."

Remember, promotion comes from the Lord. He is the one who opens doors and gives us opportunities. When we follow these Biblical steps, we are positioning ourselves for promotion from the Lord. He sees what you're doing and will reward you openly.

3

Prepared in the King's Palace

One of the young men spoke up, "I know someone. I've seen him myself: the son of Jesse of Bethlehem, an excellent musician. He's also courageous, of age, well-spoken, and good-looking. And God is with him." - 1 Samuel 16:18

When you have served in obscurity, you will be discovered by someone who will serve as a butler for your next position of promotion. They will connect you to your destiny.

David served his Heavenly Father faithfully by serving his earthly Father. This is an important principle that David practiced.

"Honor your father and mother." This is the first commandment with a promise: "so that it may go well with you and that you may enjoy long life on the earth." - Ephesians 6:3

Serving your Father prepares you.

Few men fully realize the importance of serving their earthly Father to propel them into their own. It is evident that in Jesse's household, the other sons were not busy with their Father's work. Of all of the sons, only David was working. That's why when the Prophet Samuel sought to anoint the next King of Israel, they had to wait for David to come out of the field.

My Father left my home when I was five years of age. My mother married another man. Although he was not my Father, nor did he have any natural care for me to be his son, I served his harsh leadership regardless of his dishonorable behavior.

During my childhood and teenage years, I worked for him without pay. I am not speaking about chores. I am talking about farming, ranching, and working in various businesses he owned.

Honestly, I never really thought of it in a negative sense. I learned a lot from him — what to do and what not to do. I worked faithfully, caring about doing it well and diligently in whatever task I was assigned. Of course, I wasn't perfect. I was ignorant. Unfortunately, he never taught me what to do and how to do it. He just barked out commands to get it done.

When I did leave home and embarked on my path, I was prepared with a work ethic that many of my peers lacked. This preparation propelled me in my work.

Serving another man positions you for your own.

King Saul recruited David to be his personal worship leader. When David appeared before the King, Saul liked him immediately and made him his right-hand man.

After that, whenever the bad depression from God tormented Saul, David got out his harp and played. That would calm Saul down, and he would feel better as the moodiness lifted. – 1 Samuel 16:23

David was anointed to serve.

Saul lost the anointing. Saul's only access to the anointing was vicariously through David's worship.

I've seen this so many times in men's lives. Men who have forfeited the anointing in their lives through disobedience and, at times, wickedness, and their only access point is during worship services.

David was in close harmony with the Spirit of the LORD. His songs were so anointed that he sang prophetic lyrics that the Messiah, Jesus, would live out.

Think about that. King Saul was soothed from demonic activity because of the Messianic songs that were being sung.

It was during this time that David learned about Kingdom business. He learned from King Saul what to do and, more importantly, what not to do.

Here are five biblical benefits of serving another man faithfully:

1. **You grow in your relationship with God.** When we serve, we follow in the footsteps of Jesus Christ, who came to serve, not to be served (Matthew 20:28). As we serve others, we learn more about God's love and grace, and we grow in our love for Him.

2. **You develop your character.** Serving others helps us to develop important character qualities such as humility, patience, kindness, and compassion. As we serve others, we learn to put their needs before our own and grow in our

ability to love and forgive others.

3. **You build stronger relationships.** When we serve others, we are investing in our relationships with them. We show them that we care about them and are willing to sacrifice for them. This builds trust and respect, and it leads to stronger relationships.

4. **You bring glory to God.** When we serve others faithfully, we are bringing glory to God. We are showing the world that God's love is real and powerful. We are also attracting others to Christ.

5. **You receive blessings from God.** The Bible promises that God will bless those who serve others. For example, Proverbs 11:25 says, "A generous person will prosper; whoever refreshes others will be refreshed." And Matthew 25:35-40 says that those who serve the poor and hungry, the sick and imprisoned, are serving Jesus Christ Himself.

Here are some Bible verses that support these benefits:

- **1 Corinthians 10:24** - "Let no one seek his good, but the good of his neighbor."
- **Philippians 2:3-4** - "Do nothing out of selfish ambition or vain conceit, but in humility consider others better than yourselves. Each of you should look not only to your interests but also to the interests of others."
- **Galatians 5:13** - "For you were called to freedom, brothers. Do not use your freedom as an opportunity for the flesh, but through love serve one another."
- **Matthew 6:20** - "But store up for yourselves treasures in heaven, where moth and rust do not destroy, and where thieves do not break in and steal."

- **Hebrews 13:16** – "Do not neglect to do good and to share what you have, for such sacrifices are pleasing to God."

When we serve another man faithfully, we benefit not only him but also ourselves and our relationship with God.

In my book, **The Seven Laws Which Govern Increase and Order**, I wrote a chapter on The Law of Mutual Benefit. This Law guarantees that each party in a relationship experiences an increase for themselves.

When we ask, *"What's in it for me?"* we are not speaking out of line. This question shouldn't bother an employer, nor does it intimidate God.

> *"You do not have because you do not ask God." – James 4:2*

In the context of this statement, I am assuming that you're not asking out of greed, envy, or covetousness. If you ask God from wrong motives, selfish ambition, or an unrighteous agenda, you won't receive it from Him in the first place, and if you did, you would spend it on fleshly desires.

David seizes the opportunity.

We know the story well. It is legendary. The narrative of David versus Goliath has been written countless times. I am concerned that if I start it, you will skip over this very important lesson of serving another man. So, please take time to digest the following few points of this story. I aim to bring practical principles that empower you to seize opportunities when others only see opposition.

Goliath was a champion warrior for the Philistines. The

Philistines have been a thorn in the flesh of Israel ever since they inherited the Promised Land. The Philistines are a non-Semitic people group in southern Palestine, modern Gaza. The Philistines were hostile, violent men who had migrated from southern Europe and Greece.

As a paid assassin, Goliath was noteworthy. He was a descendant of the giants — either the Nephilim, Rephaim, or Anakim. His armor was from Greece. His name is based on the Indo-European warrior-beast mythology, meaning *Lion-Man*.

Goliath was a wicked man. David's insult that Goliath was an "uncircumcised Philistine" means that he was without a covenant with God. Historically, it is said that Goliath worshiped the Philistine god, Dagon.

Goliath was a mocker.

His arrogance ridiculed the Israelite army. He taunted them, asking for a warrior of his equal to come out and fight.

Overhearing Goliath's threats, David asks, *"What will be done for the man who defeats this giant and removes this disgrace from Israel?"*

This question sparks a sharp rebuke from his angry elder brother, Eliab, saying, *"Why have you come down here? And with whom did you leave those few sheep in the wilderness? I know how conceited you are and how wicked your heart is; you came down only to watch the battle."*

Isn't it interesting how Eliab is projecting? He is attributing his own thoughts, feelings, and behavior to David. Look at how dismissive Eliab is to David.

- Why are you here?
- You are unfaithful as a shepherd.
- You're a failed leader because you did not leave the sheep

attended.
- I know how conceited you are.
- Your heart is wicked.
- You're only a spectator.

Eliab's projection is stunning since it was he who was rejected by the Spirit of the LORD after his heart was examined. It was Eliab who did not care for his father's sheep. It was Eliab that was conceited. Eliab was also the spectator to David's defeat of Goliath!

David doesn't address these slanderous accusations. He responds, *"What have I done? Is there not a cause?"*

You will discover that when you're doing something outside the norm — you will face the mockery of those unwilling to fight for the prize.

Not everyone is cut out for the high-calling of purpose.

David is motivated by his purpose.

A purpose is more significant than riches. King Saul had offered a great reward for the man who would step up to the challenges of Goliath. However, none of these rewards moved any of the fighters of Israel, including David's brothers, Eliab, Abinadab, or Shammah.

The King's reward was:

1. Great riches.
2. Tax exemption.
3. Royal Lineage.

Each of these rewards is significant for David. He would experience wealth beyond imagination for a Shepherd. He would have the financial advantage of tax exemption. But more important than the first two is the third reward, royal lineage.

The third reward would be the catalyst that moved David into the field of Elah. By marrying the King's daughter, the prophecy and anointing of his life could become a reality. He would be in the royal line of the throne. The prophecy of purpose could be fulfilled.

Crisis brings opportunity.

When you are facing a crisis or challenge, follow David's example:

1. **Use what you have proven.** Don't assume strategies or presume the experiences of others. Reading biographies and learning from men is great, but your circumstances and challenges must be faced with your proven skills.
2. **Recall past victories.** You have overcome challenges before. How did you do it? How did God help you? It may have been a smaller battle, but it was a lesson for you. It prepared you for this opportunity.
3. **Remember your position in Christ.** You have a covenant with God through Jesus Christ! You are a winner, a champion, and more than a conqueror.
4. **Don't be afraid to ask, "What will be done for the man... ?"** Any business deal has contracts of expected economic exchange for results achieved.
5. **In any endeavor, the question is not "*Can* I do it?" but "*Will* I do it?"** *Can* is an article of ability. *Will* is an article of desire, emotion, and commitment. David did not passively say that he may be able to do it; he said he can and will do it.

6. **The benefit for Israel was the defeat of their mortal enemy.** The mutual benefit for David was the reward, the positioning, and the fulfillment of his prophetic purpose and destiny.

The greatest threat to a prophesied purpose is the current comforts of your life.

I cannot tell you how many men I have seen withdraw from opportunities because they considered the reward was not worth the risk. I get that. It's challenging to leave the creature comforts of your life to pursue a higher purpose.

I have faced this dilemma multiple times in my life. Do I settle in and live out my days? Or do I take the risk to do something significant for my God? I have 'started over' these times with confidence in what I have proven but more assured that God was directing my steps.

It hasn't been easy!

Trust me. There are times when the bills are due, when you look at your investment accounts depleted and your savings accounts are drained, and wonder if you've heard from God. I have friends who questioned my sanity over it from time to time. It's not easy. Not everyone can live this way.

My journey out of comfort.

I left a very good job in the coal mine at a young age to attend Bible College. While in college, I became a sales manager at a car wash, making an unbelievable amount of money for that time. When graduating college, I left the car wash to earn a fourth of my income as a youth pastor.

The church board offered to purchase my wife and me a home

if we would commit to staying at the youth pastorate position. I declined and left to start a church with no salary or guaranteed income.

After nine years at that church, we grew in attendees, purchased 17 acres, built buildings, and started a school, leaving them with $4.7 million in assets. My departing gift was $5,000 severance pay, a fraction of what would have been the norm.

I served another man and his ministry. He paid me well as an executive. However, I did so without hesitation or calculation when the Holy Spirit told me to resign. I didn't have anywhere to go or income to have.

I started another church in a complicated city. Again, no salary. No guarantee. Nothing promised. This was a spiritual battle from day one and continued for four years. Although we saw hundreds of people make decisions for Christ and a few hundred become church members, the daily grind of spiritual warfare was taxing on me. I admit that I became harsh and hurt by the betrayal of some of my friends, especially some in my fellowship. I had my share of 'Eliabs' who called me conceited, questioned my efforts, accused me of selfish gain, and slandered my character.

When I transitioned the church to an associate, I knew that he would be a better fit for the long term. I answered every question with integrity and worked diligently to do things right. The church was not in the position to pay me deferred back pay nor pay off the credit that I had personally extended to it of more than $200,000. I choose to count it as a financial seed.

After traveling and consulting large ministries, non-profits, churches, and Christian businesses for four years, the Holy Spirit gave me this last assignment.

Starting a movement for men has been my greatest challenge

and potentially my greatest reward — not financially speaking.

FivestarMan was conceived by a Word of Knowledge. In other words, the Spirit of the LORD gave me insight and information regarding men I did not know or recognize. I suddenly had a passion and knowledgeable insight into men's purposes.

I became energetic and enthusiastic about reaching men.

After speaking to hundreds of thousands of men thirteen years later, I am more convinced than ever that I am fulfilling a prophetic purpose for my life.

I genuinely believe that every experience I had leading up to this assignment prepared me for my purpose.

I normally do not share these details in my journey, but I want to assure you that I've been there. Some men see me from a distance and never consider the price that I've paid to do what I do.

Please forgive my short journey here, but I am not embittered by it; I am emboldened to do more. My LORD has done too much for me; I can't repay. He is the Blesser, and I am the blessed.

4

Delusional Dictators

The women sang as they played and danced, saying,
"Saul has slain his thousands,
And David his ten thousands." – 1 Samuel 18:7

That song was the moment when Saul's demons were aroused against his servant David.

Fear causes delusion and phobic reactions in narcissistic and insecure men. It contorts friends into foes. The spirit of fear and timidity works in weakness, hate, and unrestrained behavior.

This is the spirit behind terrorism. A tormenting spirit that preys on weakness, causing men to assume cowardly positions. I've seen strong men take a fetal position out of fear.

Fear grips those who have a position of power but lack godly authority. Saul was in that position. He was King of Israel without the anointing for the job.

David was the man.

Think about it. How many men have songs written about

them? Especially in a good way!

The girls of Israel loved David. He was everything that they could imagine him to be — good-looking, intelligent, courageous, a warrior, wealthy, tax-exempt, anointed, and a prophesied purpose for his life.

Saul was angry and began to compare.

Comparison is deadly.

The biggest problem with comparison is that you don't believe that God is creative and resourceful enough to enlarge you while at the same time promoting others.

Here are five warnings about comparison:

1. Comparison can lead to envy and discontent. When we compare ourselves to others, we often focus on what they have that we don't. This can lead to feelings of envy and discontent. We may start to resent the other person for their success, and we may feel like we are not good enough.

2. Comparison can lead to unrealistic expectations. When we compare ourselves to others, we often set unrealistic expectations. We may think we must have the same things as others to be happy and successful. This can lead to a lot of stress and frustration.

3. Comparison can lead to low self-esteem. When we constantly compare ourselves to others, it can chip away at our self-esteem. We may start to feel like we are not good enough, smart enough, or successful enough. This can lead to a lot of negative emotions, such as anxiety, depression, and loneliness.

4. Comparison can prevent us from appreciating our unique gifts and talents. Everyone has their unique gifts and talents. When we compare ourselves to others, we may focus on what we don't have rather than what we do have. This can prevent us from appreciating our unique gifts and talents.

5. Comparison can lead us to make bad decisions. When we constantly compare ourselves to others, we may start making bad decisions to keep up. This may include spending money we don't have, getting into debt, or putting ourselves in unhealthy situations.

It is important to remember that everyone is different. We all have our unique strengths and weaknesses. We should focus on being the best version of ourselves rather than comparing ourselves to others.

Here are some tips for avoiding comparison:

- Focus on your own goals and accomplishments rather than comparing yourself to others.
- Celebrate your successes, no matter how small they may seem.
- Be grateful for what you have rather than focusing on what you don't have.
- Surround yourself with positive people who support you and make you feel good about yourself.
- Practice self-compassion and acceptance. Remember that everyone is different and that you are perfectly unique and wonderful.

Saul became delusional with his demons. Having lost the anointing to do his job, Saul relied upon his strengths and suffered from his weaknesses.

Again, in my experience, I have seen this delusion multiple times in leaders. They may have once been anointed, gifted, and purposeful, but for some reason, they have given themselves over to strife, manipulation, and authoritarian practices.

If you're going to be a leader of men, you must keep yourself pure with integrity of character. Otherwise, you will become a magnet for demonic delusions.

Darkened matter.

Those who willingly believe a lie expose their minds to darkened matter. If truth is optional, a lie becomes a tool for manipulation.

We're living in a time when lies are so typical in daily discourse that no one is shocked by them, and those spewing lies are not held accountable. Many people choose the lie because they prefer it over the truth.

Saul was a liar. Therefore, he became delusional.

Romans chapter one speaks of the time that we're living in.

> Yes, they knew God, but they wouldn't worship him as God or even give him thanks. And they began to think up foolish ideas of what God was like. As a result, their minds became dark and confused. Claiming to be wise, they instead became utter fools. And instead of worshiping the glorious, ever-living God, they worshiped idols made to look like mere people and birds and animals and reptiles.
> - Romans 1:21-23

Rather than acknowledging the truth of God, men began to have vain imaginations and craft an image of a god they would prefer. The dark matter of delusion set in, and they became confused.

Society as a whole is separating itself from Christianity. The further it departs, the more delusion it becomes. Just as the anointing departed Saul, the more demons he attracted. Demons are emboldened.

This is happening in real-time in our day of academic nonsense. Our elite schools are spewing untruths and foolish theories. Journalists have completely abandoned factual news for propaganda. Politicians have made the art of deception a blood sport, crafting dossiers and intel briefings that are nothing but nonsense. Cultural programmers rather than educators have taken over the education system. Entertainment has become full-blown psych-ops. And, of course, the gender wars of redefining male and female are nothing short of mendacious dissembling and depopulating humanity.

Never underestimate the destructive power of simple-minded men.

The destruction of humanity is underway. Don't think that I am using hyperbole. I am serious. While men passively sat in their man caves, our nemesis never stopped working his plan and infiltrating the pillars of our society.

Some elites have their annual meeting in Davos, Switzerland, and have announced delusional dictates that they want to impose on all of humanity. Better known as the Global Reset or Agenda 2030, which is the subjugation of all humanity — depopulation of 'unnecessary humans,' changing the diet from eating beef to feasting on bugs, and controlling every transaction with digital currency. They want to eliminate transportation for commoners and only be reserved for the very rich. Of course, Christianity must be eliminated or, at the very least, re-indoctrinated to embrace ungodly and wicked practices.

As I am writing this, news breaks that the Vatican will now baptize transgenders as Catholics.

Even evangelicals are transitioning their doctrine, unhitching from the 'Law' of God and embracing a grace message that celebrates homosexuals' faith. These apostates are corrupting the Gospel of Jesus Christ.

> *Now the Spirit speaketh expressly, that in the latter times, some shall **depart** from the **faith**, giving heed to seducing spirits, and doctrines of devils; speaking lies in hypocrisy; having their conscience seared with a hot iron; forbidding to marry, and commanding to abstain from meats, which God hath created to be received with thanksgiving of them which believe and know the truth. - 1 Timothy 4:1–3 (KJV)*

These doctrines of devils have merged churches with governments to impose their agenda on the serfs of humanity.

Notice what the agenda is:

1. Depart from faith.
2. Devote to seducing spirits.
3. Dedicate themselves to demonic teachings.
4. Speak lies.
5. Sear the conscience. No amount of wickedness is off-limits.
6. Eliminate marriage and family unit.

7. Change dietary norms from meats to bugs.

The global agenda will be accomplished by 'Stakeholders,' not elected officials. They want to eliminate and see no need for elections. Their delusions will be dictated to control all of humanity.

Men make plans; God's purpose prevails.
If all we do is watch the news and overconsume social media, we will be depressed by what we see happening. However, we must see what the Word of God promises about these men and their agendas.

Why are the nations so angry?
Why do they waste their time with futile plans?
The kings of the earth prepare for battle;
the rulers plot together
against the Lord
and against his anointed one.
"Let us break their chains," they cry,
"and free ourselves from slavery to God."

But the one who rules in heaven laughs.
The Lord scoffs at them. - Psalm 2:1-4

I love this Psalm. I read it daily. Many days, I read it multiple times. I love God's response.
He laughs!
When men make plans, God laughs.
All of these guys and gals that are meeting in their uppity

elitism and arrogant apostasy will soon see their fate. They will kneel before the Sovereign, the One who presides over the court of Heaven, and see the verdict of judgment on their heads.

> *Many are the plans in a man's heart, but it is the Lord's purpose that prevails. – Proverbs 19:21*

Once again, we see the failure of the confused plans of men. They will fail. It is prophesied. It doesn't surprise God. Their agenda will go the same way the Tower of Babel went, destroyed by their confusion.

> *We declare God's wisdom, a mystery that has been hidden, and that God destined for our glory before time began. None of the rulers of this age understood it, for if they had, they would not have crucified the Lord of glory. – 1 Corinthians 2:7–8*

Listen carefully. God's wisdom is incomprehensible to delusional people. If you listen to these people talk, they utter foolishness. They don't make sense. They claim to be so smart, yet they are fools.

Here are 8 Biblical examples of fools:

- **Nabal:** Nabal was a wealthy man who was foolish enough to refuse to help David, who had been protecting Nabal's sheep. This led to David and his men killing Nabal and his men. (1 Samuel 25)
- **Gehazi:** Gehazi was Elisha's servant who was foolish enough to take money from Naaman, the Syrian general

whom Elisha had healed of leprosy. This act of greed led to Gehazi being cursed with leprosy himself. (2 Kings 5)

- **Uzziah:** Uzziah was a good king of Judah who became foolish when he tried to burn incense in the temple. This task was reserved for priests, and Uzziah was punished for his disobedience with leprosy. (2 Chronicles 26)
- **The rich fool:** Jesus told a parable about a rich fool who built bigger barns to store his grain but died that night. (Luke 12:13–21)
- **The foolish virgins:** Jesus told a parable about five foolish virgins who ran out of oil for their lamps and were not allowed to enter the wedding feast. (Matthew 25:1–13)
- **The person who builds their house on sand:** Jesus told a parable about a person who built their house on sand, which was destroyed by a storm. (Matthew 7:24–27)
- **Ananias and Sapphira:** Ananias and Sapphira were a couple who lied to the Holy Spirit about the amount of money they had sold their property for. They were both struck dead for their deception. (Acts 5:1–11)
- **Demas:** Demas was a follower of Paul who abandoned him for the love of the world. (2 Timothy 4:10)

These are just a few examples of fools from the Bible. The Bible teaches us that foolishness is the opposite of wisdom and leads to sin and destruction. We should all strive to be wise and to avoid the foolishness that leads to ruin.

Here are some of the lessons we can learn from these examples:

- **Don't be selfish and greedy.** Nabal and Gehazi were both punished for their greed. Nabal lacked hospitality. Gehazi wanted to commercialize and profit off of the anointing.

- **Obey God's commands.** Uzziah was punished for disobeying God's command not to burn incense in the temple. He assumed a priestly role for which he was not qualified. Don't step out of your lane.
- **Don't be foolish with your money.** The rich fool in Jesus' parable wasted money on building bigger barns to store his grain when he should have been investing in things that would last for eternity. Don't chase material success. Focus on living significantly.
- **Don't be careless and unprepared.** The foolish virgins in Jesus' parable ran out of oil for their lamps and were prohibited from entering the wedding feast. We should all be prepared for the day when Jesus returns.
- **Build your life on a solid foundation.** The person who built their house on the sand in Jesus' parable had their house destroyed by a storm. We should all build our lives on the foundation of Jesus Christ.
- **Don't lie to the Holy Spirit.** Ananias and Sapphira were struck dead for lying to the Holy Spirit. We should always be honest with God. You can't lie in prayer.
- **Don't let the love of the world lead you away from God.** Demas abandoned Paul for the love of the world. We should always put God first in our lives.

King Saul transferred all of his antipathy toward David. David went from being a companion on the battlefield to being his competition at home.

5

Safe in the Stronghold

David left Gath and escaped to the cave of Adullam. — 1 Samuel 22

Saul feared David because the Lord was with David but had departed from Saul. He told his son, Jonathan, and all of his servants to kill David. David's success caused him paranoia.

Saul devised schemes to entrap David. Remember when David killed Goliath, one of the rewards was the hand of the King's daughter in marriage.

Yet, Saul did not keep his pledge.

> Don't settle for a payment from the King when God wants to give you the Kingdom.

Saul then schemes, instructing his attendants to speak to David privately, saying, "Look, the King likes you, and his attendants all love you; now become his son-in-law."

Saul planned to ensnare David by having him bring a hundred Philistine foreskins in exchange for his daughter's hand in marriage. Saul thought that David would die trying.

David and his men not only killed one hundred men, he doubled the effort and brought two hundred foreskins.

This time, Saul can't withdraw his reward and gives his daughter Michal to David in marriage. This again proves to be a snare; Saul sees that David wins the heart of Michal, and she loves him.

Just as David prophesied in the Valley of Elah, *"This day the Lord will deliver you into my hands, and I'll strike you down and cut off your head. This very day, I will give the carcasses of the Philistine army to the birds and the wild animals, and the whole world will know that there is a God in Israel."*

David knew his purpose wasn't just to kill Goliath. He understood the anointing was on his life to deliver Israel.

Every time that David goes out against the Philistines, he is successful.

Saul Tries to Kill David

Now, David is considered a full-blown enemy of the State. A price is on David's head. His loyal service to Saul is not honored. He is persona non grata — an unwelcomed man.

After multiple attempts on his life, David goes into hiding.

> *David left Gath and escaped to the cave of Adullam.* — 1 *Samuel* 22

Adullam is a lowland, Pine-covered hill in the land of Judah. This refuge overlooks the Elah Valley, where David fought and triumphed over Goliath.

When David walks out of the cave, he can see the scene of his victory. He had to wonder about God's plan for his life. We hear his heart in Psalm 142:1-4.

> *I cry aloud to the Lord;*
> *I lift up my voice to the Lord for mercy.*
> *I pour out before him my complaint;*
> *before him I tell my trouble.*

> *When my spirit grows faint within me,*
> *it is you who watch over my way.*
> *In the path where I walk*
> *people have hidden a snare for me.*
> *Look and see, there is no one at my right hand;*
> *no one is concerned for me.*
> *I have no refuge;*
> *no one cares for my life.*

Have you ever felt boxed in?
I have.

I know the suffocating feeling of abandonment and betrayal. No, I haven't had a King and all his administration, intelligence forces, and military resources searching for me. Still, I have faced spiritual foes with equal admin, intel, and evil weaponry.

If you're a man of God, you are facing a battle as real as David's war.

> Wars are fought in the heavens before victories are realized on the Earth.

That is why David pulled out his guitar and began to sing prophetically while secluded in the cave. Take this lesson to heart. When you're boxed in, look up.

I cry to you, Lord;
I say, "You are my refuge,
my portion in the land of the living."

Listen to my cry,
for I am in desperate need;
rescue me from those who pursue me,
for they are too strong for me.
Set me free from my prison,
that I may praise your name.
Then the righteous will gather about me
because of your goodness to me. – Psalm 142:5-7

David goes from *"no one is concerned for me; I have no refuge"* to singing, *"You are my refuge, my portion in the land of the living."*

Men, there will be times when your only option is to look up, raise your hands, and sing prophetically over yourself.

David sings, "Set me free from my prison, that I may praise your Name."

When you feel boxed in, you feel imprisoned. This is when you praise His Name. You can praise your way out of prison.

So the jailer put them into the inner dungeon and clamped their feet in the stocks.

Around midnight Paul and Silas were praying and singing hymns to God, and the other prisoners were listening.

Suddenly, there was a massive earthquake, and the prison was shaken to its foundations. All the doors immediately flew open, and the chains of every prisoner fell off!— Acts 16:24-26

After being beaten, Paul and Silas were praying and singing hymns to God. We don't know what hymn they were singing, but it could have been the lyrics of Psalm 142, *"Rescue me from those who pursue me, for they are too strong for me. Set me free from my prison, that I may praise your name."*

Another Psalm that inspired David's prophetic singing while he was in the cave of Adullam is Psalm 57.

Have mercy on me, O God, have mercy!
   I look to you for protection.
   I will hide beneath the shadow of your wings
   until the danger passes by.
   I cry out to God Most High,
   to God who will fulfill his purpose for me.
   He will send help from heaven to rescue me,
   disgracing those who hound me.Interlude
   My God will send forth his unfailing love and faithful-
ness.

I am surrounded by fierce lions
   who greedily devour human prey—
   whose teeth pierce like spears and arrows,
   and whose tongues cut like swords.

Be exalted, O God, above the highest heavens!

May your glory shine over all the earth.

My enemies have set a trap for me.
I am weary from distress.
They have dug a deep pit in my path,
but they themselves have fallen into it.Interlude

My heart is confident in you, O God;
my heart is confident.
No wonder I can sing your praises!
Wake up, my heart!
Wake up, O lyre and harp!
I will wake the dawn with my song.
I will thank you, Lord, among all the people.
I will sing your praises among the nations.
For your unfailing love is as high as the heavens.
Your faithfulness reaches to the clouds.

Be exalted, O God, above the highest heavens.
May your glory shine over all the earth. — Psalm 57:1-11

David declares, *"I cry out to God Most High, to God who will fulfill his purpose for me."*

His purpose is the constant reminder that God called him out of the shepherd's field, anointed him before his father, guided the stone from his sling, and empowered him to defeat the Philistine armies.

Five keys to David's prayer from Psalm 57:

1. **Taking refuge in God.** David begins his prayer by crying out to God for mercy and declaring that his soul trusts Him. He knows God is his only hope and refuge during his troubles (Psalm 57:1).
2. **Trusting God's promises.** David reminds God of His promises of mercy and truth. He knows that God is faithful and will keep His word, even when circumstances seem hopeless (Psalm 57:3, 10).
3. **Seeking God's help.** David asks God to deliver him from his enemies and to silence their voices. He also asks God to establish His lovingkindness and faithfulness (Psalm 57:1, 3, 9).
4. **Praising God.** Even amid his struggles, David praises God for His greatness and glory. He knows that God is worthy of all praise, regardless of what is happening in his life (Psalm 57:5, 9-11).
5. **Surrendering to God's will.** David ends his prayer by submitting to God's will and asking for His blessing. He knows that God is in control and that He will work everything out for His good (Psalm 57:7-8).

Bonus key:

1. **Praying with perseverance.** David repeats his cry for mercy several times throughout the psalm. This shows that he was truly desperate for God's help and willing to keep praying until he received it (Psalm 57:1, 3, 9).

David's prayer in Psalm 57 models how we can pray when facing difficult times. By following his example, we can learn to take refuge in God, trust His promises, seek His help, praise Him, surrender to His will, and pray with perseverance.

This is one more Psalm that David sings when he pretends to be insane in front of Abimelech. Remember, Saul is knocking on doors and killing people who assisted in David's escape. David has to flee into enemy territory to preserve his life. Now, in desperation, David takes on this persona of mental illness.

Yet, David prays, *"I prayed to the Lord, and he answered me. He freed me from all my fears."*

Free from fear.

After speaking with hundreds of thousands of men, I can tell many are overwhelmed with fear.

Fear must be focused in the right direction.

> *For the angel of the Lord is a guard;*
> *he surrounds and defends all who fear him.* — Psalm
> 34:7

David says that the angel of the Lord is his secret service.

Years ago, President George Bush invited me to a small gathering. Before he entered the room, some earnest men came in unannounced with determined steps and observant eyes. They surveilled everyone there. Suddenly, the room was silent and surreal. No one was laughing or cutting up. A sense of fear overwhelmed the atmosphere.

That is what David is describing. When the angel of the Lord shows up, you will take notice.

I have a couple of occasions when the presence of an angel or angels showed up. After experiencing it, I realized why most people drop to the ground in fear.

Recently, I was on a ministry trip without my wife, Kay,

traveling with me. She stayed at home on this particular occasion. While praying, she heard footsteps upstairs in my office/studio. She knew that I was not home. She also knew the alarm system was on, and no one else was there. She felt fear, but not the kind of terror, but of awe. The presence of God was in the house.

Jesus admonished, *"Do not be afraid of those who kill the body but cannot kill the soul. Rather, be afraid of the One who can destroy both soul and body in hell."* (Matthew 10:28)

Men, you do not have to fear this world or any actors in play right now! These schemers do not have power over us. They can't destroy us.

Go to God and draw your strength from Him. Then, turn and strengthen your family.

5 Biblical keys to overcoming fear of men:

1. **Know that God is greater than any man.** When we fear men, we are essentially saying that they have more power over us than God does. But the Bible tells us that God is the supreme ruler of the universe and that He is sovereign over all things, including the hearts of men (Psalm 95:3, Proverbs 21:1). When we remember who God is and how great He is, it helps us to put our fear of men into perspective.

2. **Trust in God's protection.** The Bible promises that God will protect those who trust in Him (Psalm 91:4, Proverbs 3:5-6). When we are afraid of men, we can remind ourselves that God is our protector and will not let any harm come to us.

3. **Stand up for what is right, even when it is difficult.** The

Bible tells us to be courageous and to stand up for what is right, even when it is difficult (Ephesians 6:10-18, 1 Peter 3:14). When we fear men, we may be tempted to compromise our convictions or to avoid standing up for what is right. But the Bible teaches us that we should always obey God, even if it means facing opposition from men.

4. **Recognize that men are only human.** It is important to remember that men are only human and just as flawed and imperfect as we are. Putting men on a pedestal makes them seem more intimidating and powerful than they really are. But when we recognize that men are just like us, it helps us to lose our fear of them.

5. **Pray for courage and wisdom.** The Bible tells us to pray for everything (Philippians 4:6). If we are struggling with fear of men, we can pray for God to give us courage and wisdom. He can help us to see the situation from His perspective and to make the right decisions.

Following these Biblical keys can overcome our fear of men and live in freedom and confidence.

The Spirit of the Lord speaking through Psalm 34 invites us to Him, and He will teach us to fear the Lord. He asks, *"Does anyone want to live a life that is long and prosperous?"*

David says we should search for peace and work to maintain it.

It's essential to take note of this, especially at a time when there is so much chaos and confusion. You can't open social media without being invited to a party of strife.

You must avoid being entrapped by division. Division starts with an offense.

> Whatever it takes to offend you is all it takes to defeat you.

Here are seven steps in the strategy to divide:

- **Offense murmurs**
- **murmuring becomes strife**
- **strife takes evil action**
- **evil action uses manipulation**
- **manipulation becomes witchcraft**
- **witchcraft rebels**
- **rebellion divides**
- **Division destroys**

Choose to walk in peace.

David decided to leave in peace rather than live in strife.

Jesus promises us peace of mind and heart. Remember, the heart is the residence of our purpose, appetites, passions, and courage.

> *"I am leaving you with a gift—**peace** of mind and heart. And the **peace** I give is a gift the **world** cannot give. So don't be troubled or afraid. — John 14:27*

David concludes Psalm 34 with this powerful statement, "No one who takes refuge in Him will be condemned."

6

Gathering the Outcasts

All those who were in distress or in debt or discontented gathered around him, and he became their commander. About four hundred men were with him. — 1 Samuel 22:2

Society can be brutal. Especially when a wicked and delusional leader is chasing down innocent men as King Saul was doing in Israel. However, David wasn't alone in his fight for justice. There were at least four hundred men who were also seeking refuge.

The Cave of Adullam became a gathering place for those society had cast out. All who were distressed, in debt, or discontented gathered at the stronghold.

The word Adullam means justice for men.

The men who gathered at the Adullam were hurt and seeking their revenge. Wounded men are dangerous. Like a caged animal, rage is in control.

Distress

Earlier, we talked about feeling boxed in. That is what distress means. It is confinement, anguish, every man in straits.

Experiencing distress is a normal human response to challenging or difficult situations. It can trigger a range of emotions, both positive and negative. Here are five common emotional reactions to being in distress:

1. **Fear:** Fear is a natural response to perceived threats or danger. When we are distressed, our bodies go into "fight-or-flight" mode, which can cause us to feel anxious, panicked, or afraid.
2. **Anger:** Anger is often a secondary emotion that arises from fear or frustration. When we are distressed, we may feel angry at the situation, at ourselves, or others.
3. **Sadness:** Sadness is a typical response to loss or disappointment. We may feel overwhelmed with sadness, grief, or despair when distressed.
4. **Guilt:** Guilt can arise from feeling responsible for the situation causing distress. We may feel guilty about our actions, inaction, or inability to control the situation.
5. **Shame:** Shame is a feeling of worthlessness or inadequacy. When distressed, we may feel ashamed of our situation, emotions, or perceived shortcomings.

Look no further than recent events around the globe. The world is in distress, from political chaos, confusion, and collaborated crises to the horrific events in the Middle East. A quick scroll on social platforms reveals people's stress, and it's not good.

In debt.

Add to the social and political climate the enormous stress people feel with their debt load. Credit Card debt has topped $1 Trillion for the first time in history. The young are grappling with Student Loans that have restricted their ability to move on toward what used to be the 'American Dream' — owning personal property like a home.

The elephant in the room is unrestrained spending by the Federal Government. Budget Deficiencies are record high. National Debt is soaring, exceeding $34 Trillion. Our debt-to-national-product is now 129%.

Men, we carry this load on our shoulders because we are responsible for providing for our families — their needs and desires. We also profoundly desire to finance our purpose in life.

I am not legalistic regarding debt-free living, but I also believe we must be good stewards of our leverage. I have found two teachers and their resources beneficial regarding financial stewardship, Dave Ramsey and Gary Keesee.

Dave Ramsey's baby step program is a 7-step plan to help people escape debt and build wealth. It is a simple and effective plan that has helped millions achieve their financial goals.

Here are the seven baby steps, simplified:

1. **Save $1,000 for an emergency fund.** This will give you a cushion to fall back on in case of unexpected expenses.
2. **Pay off all debt (except the house) using the debt snowball method.** This means paying off the smallest debt first, then the next smallest, and so on. This method can help you stay motivated and make progress quickly.
3. **Save 3-6 months of expenses in a fully funded emergency**

fund. Once you have paid off all of your debt, except for your house, you should save 3-6 months of expenses in an emergency fund. This will give you peace of mind and help you avoid going into debt again in case of a job loss or other unexpected event.

4. **Invest 15% of your household income in retirement.** This will help you ensure that you have enough money saved for retirement. The sooner you start investing, the more time your money has to grow.

5. **Save for your children's college fund.** This will help you offset college costs and make it more affordable for your children.

6. **Pay off your house early.** This will save you a significant amount of money in interest.

7. **Build wealth and give.** You can start giving back to others once you have reached your financial goals.

The baby step program is a proven way to achieve financial success. It is essential to stick with the plan and be patient. It may take some time, but it will be worth it.

I also mentioned Gary Keesee. His ministry, Fixing the Money Thing, is helping tens of thousands with establishing a faith journey with their finances. I really like his practical yet faith-filled teachings.

Discontent

This word is *mar*, which means bitterness, pain, and chafed. I have met countless men who have swallowed bitter roots.

See to it that no one falls short of the grace of God and

that no bitter root grows up to cause trouble and defile many. —Hebrews 12:15

When someone is discontent, they chew on bitter morsels. You can smell the acidity and hear the bitterness in their words. It is very similar to acid reflux. It is poisoned regurgitation.

Again, this is the culture of our time. Men are discontent. In my lifetime, I've never seen our nation at this level of discontent. A recent Pew Research discovered that just 4% of U.S. adults say the political system is working well. (Pew Research Center, September 19, 2023)

Every negative can be redirected into a positive. That is the definition of repentance, the turning of the mind.

Discontentment can be a powerful motivator. It can drive you to achieve great things if you channel it correctly.

Repentance is to change the mind. Change is hard. However, as John Maxwell points out, people will change if they are discontent enough.

When they hurt enough, they have to.
When they see enough, they are inspired too.
When they learn enough, they want to.
When they receive enough, they are able to. - Dr. John Maxwell

Here are five keys to turning discontentment into success:

1. Identify the source of your discontentment. The first step to turning discontentment into success is to identify what is causing you to feel this way. Are you unhappy with your job?

Your relationship? Your health? Once you know what is making you unhappy, you can start to take steps to address it.

2. Set goals for yourself. Once you know what you want to change, you need to set some goals for yourself. What do you want to achieve? What kind of life do you want to live? Setting goals will give you something to strive for and help you stay motivated.

3. Take action. Don't just sit around and complain about your situation. Take action to make things better. This could involve changing your lifestyle, starting a new job, or ending a relationship.

4. Be patient. Change takes time. Don't expect to see results overnight. Keep putting in the effort, and you will eventually reach your goals.

5. Celebrate your successes. When you achieve a goal, no matter how small, take some time to celebrate. This will help you stay motivated and keep moving forward.

It is important to remember that discontentment is not always a bad thing. It can be a sign that you are ready for change and growth. If you can positively channel your discontentment, it can be a powerful force for good in your life.

Every gathering of men requires a leader.

As these four hundred men gathered to David, they considered him their leader. You can imagine the cave's atmosphere with that many men are distressed, in debt, and discontent. It certainly wasn't a motivational seminar!

David's journey to the King's Palace is well underway. However, at this point, in the cave of Adullam, it doesn't look promising. The only indication that things will turn around is the promises of prophecy that David received.

There will be times when you only have the promises of God to sustain you.

Listen carefully.

This is very important.

The Word of God will give you the tenacity to fulfill your purpose.

You must develop a reliance on the Word of God over all things. His promises are true. His character is flawless. He is not a man that He can lie.

From my experience, I have discovered that my daily reading of Scripture is how I have maintained my tenacity to fulfill my purpose.

Here are five key disciplines to read the Word of God:

1. Set aside dedicated time for reading.

Just like any other important activity, reading the Bible requires dedicated time. Make it a habit to set aside time each day to read and study the Scriptures. Even if it's just for 15 or 20 minutes, regular time in the Word will make a significant difference in your spiritual growth. By reading 45 minutes daily, I can read through the Bible every 90 days. I use YouVersion.com reading plans to track my reading. Start with **TheDailyChampion.com** to have a devotional and read one chapter of Proverbs daily.

2. Choose a translation that suits your understanding.

Many Bible translations are available, each with its style and language. Take some time to explore other translations and find one that you can easily understand and enjoy reading. Don't get tripped up by arguments over translations. I read dozens of translations. I check all translations by reading the original languages to gain the whole meaning of the Scriptures.

3. Read with a focus on understanding and application.

Don't just read the Bible to check off a box. Take the time to understand what you're reading. Ask yourself questions like: What does this passage mean? How does it apply to my life? You will notice that all of our FivestarMan Field Notes are designed on the Purpose, Precept, Principle, and Practice. In other words, what is the purpose of this writing? What does this Scripture establish as a universal, unchangeable truth? What is the understanding and application of this precept? And how can I put this precept and principle into practice?

4. Use study tools and resources.

Many great tools and resources are available to help you study the Bible. Commentaries, study guides, and online resources can provide valuable insights and help you understand the context of the Scriptures. You must be careful to realize that commentary is often biased opinion and sectarian doctrine. It's important to rely on the Scripture more than the commentary of the Scripture.

5. Engage in a small group or find a mentor.

Reading the Bible with others can enhance your understanding and provide encouragement and support. It is essential to have a small gathering of men so that you can read and study the Word of God together. Men are primarily looking for strategy over emotive from the Word of God. We will talk more about this soon.

Remember, reading the Bible is not a race or a chore. It's an opportunity to connect with God and grow your relationship. Take your time, savor the words, and allow God to speak to you through His Word.

FivestarMan Engage

To answer the need for men to engage with one another, at FivestarMan, we provide a weekly live stream to engage men, mentoring men individually and in small groups in churches across the nations, including Chile and Brazil.

David began to sing his prophetic songs.

The impact of singing the Word is corporate. Men must come together and encounter God, so much so that God instructed Moses to gather the men three times per year to encounter The best practices of men's ministries, including unique corporate gatherings with a rhythm of three to four times yearly.

We call these FivestarMan Encounters. We keep it simple: singing in praise and worship, typically anthem, arousing and uplifting, and declarative songs. We also recommend repentant worship songs and not overusing romantic worship songs.

I strongly encourage the men that they will see corresponding benefits to these FivestarMan Encounters:

1. God will give you authority over principalities, powers, and authorities;
2. God will defend your marriage, family, and possessions.
3. God will promote you and increase your business.
4. God will protect your property from loss and seizure.

Every week, I encourage men on our social platforms with an image that has reached millions.

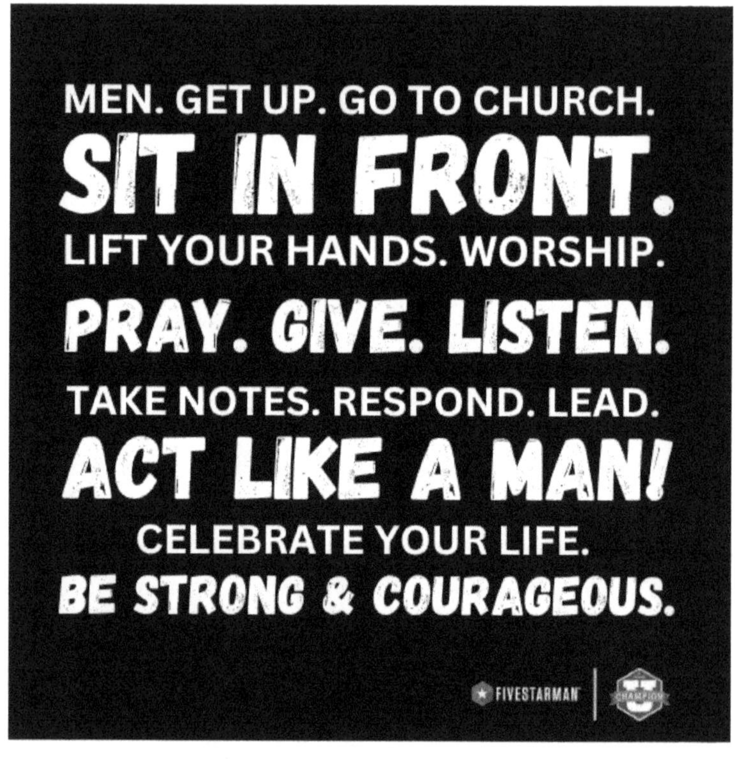

It's time that men step into leadership. Being spiritual is not reserved for females. Men are spiritual. It's time that we show it.

Men should be closer to the altar than they are to the exit.

Before David could turn these men into warriors, he first had to turn them into worshipers.

7

From Passivity to Purpose

One day the prophet Gad told David, "Leave the stronghold and return to the land of Judah." —1 Samuel 22:5

David is preparing the four hundred men. He is establishing them in the Word and worship. Then, he does something that many people overlook. David takes his family to a secure location in Moab. He makes arrangements with the King of Moab, saying, *"Please take care of my father's household and let them stay with you until I learn what God will do with me?"*

Before God moves you, you must make a move of preparation.

I've known so many men who remain in passivity, awaiting a word from the Lord but never taking the initiative to be ready to hear from the Lord. Men waste so much time, energy, and resources — often missing the moment of opportunity and forfeiting their chance to do something.

God orders your steps, but you must be the one who takes them.

Are you ready?

Suppose I came to you and offered an all-expense vacation to the most amazing destination imaginable but with a catch. You only have three days before you leave. Are you ready?

Would you be able to pull it off?

Are you prepared?

Paul told his protege, Timothy, *"Be ready in season and out of season!"*

So many men miss their season of opportunity.

I have.

I was invited to the table, so to speak, with an enormous opportunity. A man of significant influence escorted me into the room, which had the potential for me to reach hundreds of thousands of men. The position itself held enormous influence. Although the Lord may have been protecting me and our efforts at FivestarMan, I reflect on it with a sigh of disappointment. Did I miss it? Was I prepared for it? Was I too naive?

Maybe.

Success is when preparation meets opportunity.

Opportunities often arise unexpectedly, but being prepared can significantly increase your chances of success when they do.

Here are five ways to position yourself for opportunities:

1. Cultivate self-awareness:

- Identify your strengths, weaknesses, interests, and values.
- Understand your career goals and aspirations.
- Reflect on your past experiences and accomplishments.

Self-awareness helps you recognize opportunities that align with your skills and aspirations, making you more likely to seize them effectively. If it doesn't align with your purpose, it is a distraction.

2. Continuously learn and upskill:

- Stay updated on trends and advancements.
- Develop new skills that complement your existing expertise.
- Expand your knowledge base through courses, certifications, or online resources.
- Be a lifelong learner.
- Read. Read. Read.

Continuous learning demonstrates your commitment to personal and professional growth, making you a valuable asset to potential opportunities. Don't have nostalgia for the good old days of ignorance.

3. Build a strong network:

- Connect with professionals in your field and related industries.
- Engage in industry events, conferences, and workshops.
- Leverage online platforms to expand your network.
- Learn the social media game. It's a love/hate relationship. Use it to your advantage. Don't get distracted by the noise. Just because someone has a voice doesn't mean you must listen to them.
- Learn the art of blocking, deleting, unfriending, and canceling.

Networking broadens your connections, increases your visibility, and opens doors to potential opportunities.

4. Seek feedback and mentorship:

- Seek guidance from experienced mentors or career counselors.
- Request constructive feedback from colleagues and supervisors.
- Participate in performance reviews and self-evaluations.
- Especially ask the Holy Spirit to counsel you. He will advise you at night if you will ask Him. (Psalm 16:7)

Feedback and mentorship help you identify areas for improvement and refine your skills, making you better prepared for opportunities.

5. Be proactive and seize initiative:

- Step up. Volunteer for challenging projects or assignments.

- Seek out opportunities to demonstrate your leadership skills.
- Do not fear failure.
- Take initiative to solve problems and contribute to your organization.

Proactiveness showcases your willingness to take on new challenges and your commitment to excellence, making you stand out as a candidate for opportunities.

God uses prophets.

He still does. Prophets are inspired men. They receive spiritual messages, much like an angel or messenger; however, they are human. When God wants to deliver a message, He sends an *nāḇā'*, pronounced naw–bee' named Gad, to the recipient. Gad means 'good fortune.'

Some scholars attribute the Books of Samuel to the prophet Gad. God uses Gad as David's personal prophet. Here, in 1 Samuel 22 and later, David sins by taking a census of the people of Israel and Judah.

Think about it this way: the prophet 'Good Fortune' comes to the cave and speaks a message inspired by the Spirit of the Lord. The message is short and sweet, *"Leave the stronghold and return..."*

I can speculate another way of saying, "David, you can't fulfill your purpose while hiding in the cave. Don't let this stronghold become too comfortable for you. Don't allow passivity to paralyze you from your purpose."

This is the message that I bring to men everywhere that I go.

I may not be a prophet, nor the son of a prophet, but I do have an inspired message to speak to men, *"Men, God has bigger plans for you than being seduced by the sofa, too comfortable on the couch, watching yard games on television and playing fantasy games!"*

I've offended a lot of men with these words. I've had letters written and certified delivered to my ministerial overseers. I wounded the sensitivities of feminized men. But with all sincerity of heart, I know that God wants you not to sit down while the world is in chaos, confusion, and a crisis of sin.

> **"Men, God has bigger plans for you than being seduced by the sofa, too comfortable on the couch, watching yard games on television, and playing fantasy games!"**

Proverbs says, *"Wounds from a friend can be trusted."* I am certainly not trying to hurt someone. But I've learned that you can't trust someone to be loyal if they are not honest with you first.

Breaking free from stagnation and regaining momentum can be challenging, but it's definitely possible with the right approach. Here are five key strategies to help you get back on track:

1. **Identify the root cause of your stagnation:** Before you can start moving forward, it's essential to understand what's holding you back. Are you feeling overwhelmed by too much on your plate? Are you lacking motivation or direction? Once you identify the source of your stagnation, you can address it directly.

2. **Set small, achievable goals:** Trying to tackle everything at once can quickly lead to overwhelm and discouragement. Instead, break down your larger goals into smaller, more

manageable steps. This will make the tasks seem less daunting and give you a sense of accomplishment as you progress.

3. **Create a structured routine:** A lack of structure can contribute to feelings of stagnation and inertia. Establish a daily or weekly routine that includes time for work, personal activities, and relaxation. Having a schedule can help you stay focused and productive.

4. **Challenge yourself and step outside your comfort zone:** Stagnation often occurs when we get too comfortable in our routines. To break free from this pattern, consciously challenge yourself and step outside your comfort zone. This could involve taking on new projects, learning new skills, or trying new things.

5. **Seek support from others:** Don't hesitate to reach out for help from friends, family, or a professional if you're struggling to regain momentum. A support system can provide encouragement, motivation, and fresh perspectives.

Remember, progress is not always linear, and there will be setbacks along the way. Be patient with yourself, celebrate your accomplishments, and keep moving forward. With consistent effort and the right strategies, you can overcome stagnation and regain momentum in your life.

FivestarMan ChampionU.Life

We launched ChampionU.Life so men would have intentional direction in their pursuit of Biblical/Authentic manhood. Tens of thousands of men have initiated the steps of their personalized journey.

We've worked hard to aggregate three journeys of five sets

of video teachings, each with at least five lessons. We're continuously improving and adding more content to empower men.

Get started by going to FivestarMan.com. When you do, I will give you a free digital copy of my book, FIVESTARMAN, a copy of the 45 Day Challenge Field Guide, a video series, The Five Passions of Authentic Manhood, and deliver to you, TheDailyChampion.com.

When you complete The Five Passions of Authentic Manhood, you can continue your pursuit with ChampionU.Life.

After David secures his father in Moab, he hears the inspired message from the prophet Gad, ***"Time to leave the cave."***

8

The Field of Contest

> *When David was told, "Look, the Philistines are fighting against Keilah and are looting the threshing floors," he inquired of the Lord, saying, "Shall I go and attack these Philistines?"* —1 Samuel 23:1-2

This is one of the most interesting passages that I have studied. It will destroy a lot of people's speculation about how God works in their lives regarding decisions and destiny. Paying attention to what happens could change how we respond to what we hear from the Lord.

The Old Testament stories serve as examples for us.

> *These things happened to them as examples and were written down as warnings for us on whom the culmination of the ages has come.* —1 Corinthians 10:11

David receives reports of the Philistines terrorizing and looting Keilah. This city is known as the Citadel, a fortress in Judah's lowlands. His purpose calls David to ask the Lord, "Should I go and attack the Philistines?"

Not every fight is worthy of you.

We must learn to inquire of God to determine our fights. If you don't know the right thing to fight for, you will find the wrong things to fight against. If it does not align with your purpose, it is a distraction.

The Lord answered David, "Go, attack the Philistines and save Keilah."

This word has more information than at first glance. The Lord confirms David's desire to defend the Philistines. The Lord also affirms that David will save Keilah.

I've learned to carefully meditate on every word I've heard from the Lord. There have been many times that I've rehearsed what I've listened to and reread what I've recorded in my journals to discover hidden nuggets of truth that I may have missed earlier.

When David tells his Champions — the Mighty Men of David — they are yet convinced that this is a good idea. They don't have complete confidence in David's ability to hear from the Lord and lack self-confidence in their ability to fight. Remember, these are the same distressed, in debt, and discontented men of earlier.

David returns to the Lord and inquires of Him. The Lord confirms, "Go down to Keilah; I will give the Philistines into your hand."

**A leader doesn't take people where they want to go.
A leader takes them where they are supposed to go.**

Guiding people toward a destination that may not align with their immediate desires requires dedicated leadership with confidence. Here are five key strategies for leaders to effectively navigate this process:

1. **Establish a Clear Vision and Purpose:** Articulate a compelling vision that inspires and motivates individuals to see the value of the journey ahead. Clearly define the purpose and desired outcomes, ensuring everyone understands the significance of the direction being taken.
2. **Give faith-to-follow:** They must hear from you. You've heard from God and have His Word, which has assured you the decision. Now, you must turn and strengthen them to follow. Recognize and acknowledge individuals' perspectives, concerns, and potential resistance to change. Show empathy for their viewpoints and create a safe space for open communication. David communicated with his Champions.
3. **Effective Communication:** Engage in transparent and consistent communication, keeping everyone informed about the reasons behind the change, the progress being made, and any challenges encountered. Address concerns promptly and openly.
4. **Encourage Participation and Ownership:** Foster a culture of collaboration and participation. Involve individuals in decision-making processes and give them ownership of

specific tasks or contributions. Empower them to take the initiative and contribute their unique perspectives.

5. **Celebrate Successes and Milestones:** Recognize and celebrate achievements along the way, no matter how small. Positive reinforcement and acknowledgment of progress will boost morale and maintain motivation.

Remember, leading people to a destination they may not initially desire is not about forcing compliance or imposing intimidation. It's about inspiring them to see the bigger picture, understanding the benefits of the change, and empowering them to contribute to the collective success. By employing these strategies, leaders can effectively guide their teams toward a brighter future, even if it requires a change in direction.

The field of contest.

So David and his Champions went to Keilah, defeated the Philistines, gained livestock as a bounty reward, and saved the citizens of the Citadel.

News about this event reached the ears of King Saul. Saul is so delusional that he believes that God has delivered David into his hands, entrapping David in the Citadel. Saul rallies his forces to seize David finally.

> **Enemies look for openings, deceptions, distractions, and entrapment.**

We need to be very careful when facing opposition. Don't be naive to think that your enemy has any moral code of conduct or rational thoughts of God. The demons have enticed Saul's delusional brain to believe that he is doing the bidding of God.

> *They will put you out of the synagogue; in fact, the time is coming when anyone who kills you will think they are offering a service to God. —John 16:2*

When I was young and naive, I thought those who do evil know they are doing evil. Now, I realize those who do evil think they are offering a service to God.

God gives foreknowledge of something that doesn't happen.

> *David said, "Lord, God of Israel, your servant has heard definitely that Saul plans to come to Keilah and destroy the town on account of me. Will the citizens of Keilah surrender me to him? Will Saul come down, as your servant has heard? Lord, God of Israel, tell your servant."*
> *And the Lord said, "He will."*
> *Again David asked, "Will the citizens of Keilah surren-der me and my men to Saul?"*
> *And the Lord said, "They will."*

You may want to read that passage again.
    It is stunning.

David asked, "Lord, I've heard that Saul plans to come to Keilah and destroy the town because of me. Will the citizens surrender me to him?
    "Will Saul do this?"
    The Lord says, "Yes, He will."
    "Will the citizens hand me over to him?"

The Lord says, "Yes, they will."

So what does David do?

He leaves.

God is giving David insight into something that doesn't happen.

This is wisdom. It is knowing the outcome of a decision. David inquires of God to know the future events if he makes one decision over another.

Foreknowledge doesn't equal God's will.

This is what most men fail to realize. Just because God knows something doesn't mean that it is His will. There is a difference between faith and fate. We are men of faith, not fate.

Faith and fate are two concepts that are often confused with each other, but they have distinct meanings and implications.

Here are five key distinctions between faith and fate:

1. Nature: Faith is a belief or conviction, while fate is a predetermined course of events. Faith is an active choice to believe in something, while fate is a passive acceptance of what will happen.

2. Evidence: Faith is often based on personal experiences, spiritual belief systems, or trust in God, while fate is often based on the idea of predestination or inevitability without your involvement. Faith's evidence is a substance of believing God's Word. It provides a sense of meaning and purpose; while fate may be seen as an external force beyond one's control, random, indeterminable events control you.

3. Role of Choice: Faith emphasizes the role of choice and personal responsibility, as it involves the decision to believe in something and act accordingly. Fate, on the other hand, suggests that events are predetermined and that individuals have little or no control over their own destiny. You're just a player in the theatre of the universe.

4. Focus: Faith is typically focused on the present and future, as it involves trust in God to continue to participate and guide your decisions actively. Fate, on the other hand, is often associated with the past and a sense of inevitability.

5. Emotional Impact: Faith can provide hope, comfort, and strength, allowing individuals to trust in something greater than themselves. On the other hand, fate can lead to feelings of resignation, powerlessness, or even despair, as it suggests that one's future is already determined.

In summary, faith is a belief system that emphasizes trust, choice, and personal responsibility, while fate is a concept that suggests predetermined events and a lack of control. Understanding the distinctions between these two concepts can help individuals navigate their own lives and make decisions that align with their values and beliefs.

> *David stayed in the wilderness strongholds and in the hills of the Desert of Ziph. Day after day Saul searched for him, but God did not give David into his hands. —1 Samuel 23:14*

Saul is relentless. Even after the constant confusion and running around chasing after David, he won't relent. Saul is exposed to David on two occasions when David could have easily killed him, seizing the Kingship of Israel; however, David was guided by both purpose and principles.

You can't allow your life's purpose to trump the principles that guide you.

Aligning your purpose with principles provides a strong foundation for making decisions, navigating challenges, and maintaining a consistent sense of direction.

Here are five reasons why principles must guide your purpose:

1. **Clarity and Focus:** Principles provide a clear framework for defining and understanding your purpose. They serve as guiding lights illuminating the path ahead, helping you stay focused on what is truly important and meaningful to you.

2. **Decision-Making Compass:** When faced with difficult decisions, your principles act as a compass, helping you make choices that align with your core values and beliefs. They provide a benchmark for evaluating options and ensuring your actions are consistent with your overall purpose.

3. **Integrity and Authenticity:** Staying true to your principles fosters integrity and authenticity. It allows you to act by following your values, even when challenging or unpopular. This builds trust and credibility, both within yourself and with others.

4. **Resilience and Adaptability:** Principles provide a foundation of resilience in facing challenges and setbacks. They remind you of your core beliefs and values, helping you persevere through difficult times and maintain a sense of direction.

5. **Continuous Growth and Evaluation:** Principles have eternal value. That's why reading Proverbs each day is still relevant for you today. They provide a framework for

constant self-reflection and improvement, allowing you to refine your purpose and adapt to changing circumstances.

You create a road map for a fulfilling and meaningful life by aligning your purpose with principles. Principles provide clarity, guidance, and resilience, enabling you to make decisions, navigate challenges, and continuously grow as an individual. Embrace the power of principles and let them guide you toward a life of purpose and fulfillment.

Remember, David was anointed to be King of Israel. He received the word of Prophet Samuel that the throne was his to sit upon. Yet, David would never dethrone Saul in order to take it.

I can't tell you how many times I have seen talented and anointed young men forfeit their future because they grasped for position rather than have God give the promotion.

> *In your relationships with one another, have the same mindset as Christ Jesus:*
> *Who, being in very nature God,*
> *did not consider equality with God something to be used to his own advantage;*
> *rather, he made himself nothing*
> *by taking the very nature of a servant,*
> *being made in human likeness.*
> *And being found in appearance as a man,*
> *he humbled himself*
> *by becoming obedient to death—*
> *even death on a cross!*

> *Therefore God exalted him to the highest place... —*

Philippians 2:5-9

This doxology is one of the best synopsis of what Jesus did. Based on Philippians 2:5-11, here are five attributes of Jesus' attitude:

1. **Humility:** Jesus humbled himself by becoming human and taking on the form of a servant. He did not cling to his equality with God but instead made himself lower than his angels, even to the point of death on the cross. (Philippians 2:6-8)
2. **Obedience:** Jesus was obedient to his Father, even to the point of death. He did not come to earth to do his own will but to do the will of his Father, who sent him. (Philippians 2:8)
3. **Selflessness:** Jesus was selfless. He did not put his own will ahead of the Father's purpose. He endured the cross because of the joy that lay upon completing it. He was willing to give up his life for those he loved. (Philippians 2:5-8)
4. **Love:** Jesus is the perfect example of love. God is love. He loved everyone, even while we were yet sinners. He taught his followers to love one another, even as he loved them. (Philippians 2:9-11)
5. **Service:** Jesus was a servant-leader. He came to earth to serve others, not to be served. He washed his disciples' feet and taught them to serve one another. (Philippians 2:7)

These five attributes are a powerful example for us all. We can strive to be more like Jesus by being humble, obedient, selfless, loving, and serving.

Here are some examples of how we can apply these attributes to our own lives:

- **Humility:** Aligning our will with God's purpose for our lives is an act of humility. It demonstrates His Lordship over our lives. Many men never actually surrender their lives to the Lordship of Jesus. When we do, we will better understand our purpose and, with joy, reach our potential.
- **Obedience:** We can obey God by following his commands and doing what is right, even when it is difficult. Obedience is a type of humility. It is denying ourselves, our cravings, our desires for what God has instructed us. Obedience is a promotion agent in our lives.
- **Selflessness:** We can be selfless by putting the needs of others before our own and giving generously to others. A generous man prospers. What you do for others, God will do for you.
- **Love:** When men show love, it may not be an eruption of emotion. Hard work, protection, provision, and reliability often demonstrate it. We can be loving by being kind and compassionate to others, even when they are challenging to love.
- **Service:** As a man, we are designed to lead. However, our leadership is based on the

Therefore God exalted him to the highest place... — Philippians 2:5-9

This is the key to promotion in the Kingdom of God. The world operates on the opposite system.

If we're going to be acknowledged in the Kingdom of God, it

will come from our servant leadership, not from intimidation and domination.

These are the qualities that men need to lead other men.

91

9

Mentoring Men

When David and his men reached Ziklag, they found it destroyed by fire and their wives and sons and daughters taken captive. So David and his men wept aloud until they had no strength left to weep. David's two wives had been captured—Ahinoam of Jezreel and Abigail, the widow of Nabal of Carmel. David was greatly distressed because the men were talking of stoning him; each one was bitter in spirit because of his sons and daughters. But David found strength in the Lord his God. —1 Samuel 30:3–6

Under David's leadership, the Champions, the former distressed, in debt, and discontented men, are now winning in life. They are prospering with each attack against the enemies of Israel. They are successfully escaping the clutches of King Saul. They are gaining wives and children. They're enjoying the fruit of under the anointed leadership of David.

Then Ziklag.

During David's run from King Saul, he lived in the Philistine territory and served King Achish of Gath. Because David went to King Achish, Saul stopped his pursuit of David.

King Achish gave to David the town of Ziklag. He established a home for himself, his 600 men, and their wives. It would serve as a base camp.

While David and his Champions are campaigning, the Amalekites raided Ziklag. They burned it, taking captive the women and children. However, they did not kill anyone.

When they returned and saw the devastation, David and his men wept. David was greatly distressed because his men were now murmuring against him and plotting to stone him.

As you step into leadership, you will discover an unfortunate reality: leadership can be lonely.

These men who were once the down-and-outers of society are now considering stoning the very one who made them the up-and-comers.

It all began with murmuring.

The seven steps to division:

- **Murmuring:** Murmuring is a muttered complaint voiced to peers, not to leaders. It is a childish response akin to a crying child who is not getting his way. When Jesus heard people murmuring, He said, *"Stop grumbling among yourselves."* (John 6:43)
- **Strife:** When a murmur is unanswered, the complainers will become contentious. They will be argumentative and irrational. For where envying and strife are, there is confusion

and every evil work. (James 3:16)

- **Evil Work**: At this point, the complaints will become active hostility against leadership. Demonic spirits are invited into the confusion.
- **Manipulation:** The demonic influences start a whispering campaign to influence someone to do something they would not otherwise do. This can be done through various tactics, such as pressure, intimidation, guilt, gas-lighting, or flattery.
- **Witchcraft:** Witchcraft is not just an old hag stirring concoctions in her cast iron pot. It is a type of prayer and worship. Not to God but to demons. It involves worship and singing enchantments. The end goal is to entice demons against leadership!
- **Rebellion:** Rebellion is the sin of witchcraft. (1 Samuel 15:23). This is precisely what the prophet Samuel tells King Saul. This is the same path Saul took that divided him from the anointing and leadership of God.
- **Division:** At this point, the agreement is severed completely. There is no longer unity or cooperation. Agreement makes two become one. Division makes one become two. This happens in divorce; God joined together, and man separated. This is what happens to teams, companies, or even churches.

Unfortunately, as a young pastor, my nativity of leadership caught me off guard. I had a team working for me.

Together, we were growing a great church and seeing God do amazing things in our midst. That was until one of my staff members swallowed a bitter morsel against me. He desired everything that I had. Then he began a murmuring campaign against me.

I learned valuable lessons about leadership by observing the tactics of our enemy.

- Enemies look for openings, deceptions, distractions, and entrapment.
- Enemies do not live by a moral code; however, they expect you to live by yours.
- Enemies will attempt to distract you from your purpose by getting you to engage in smaller, unnecessary battles.
- Your enemy will use an entry point through someone whom you trust.
- Someone you trust trusts someone who wouldn't.
- Enemies use the scheme of the question; rather than asking a question to obtain information, they ask a question to suggest doubt about your character.
- Your enemy will interpret an attack against you as a forfeiture of God's grace upon your life.
- Your enemy will attempt to isolate you from your support team.
- An enemy doesn't look to understand you; he simply wants to discredit you.
- Your enemy will speak of your pride while falsely presenting themselves in humility.
- They do not want you removed; they want you destroyed.
- They will act with mystery. They will not present evidence, only suggesting that they have it but can't share it.

My prayer during this time was **Psalm 25:21**, *"Let integrity and uprightness guard me, for my hope is in the Lord."*

I weathered the storm. I protected the congregation. I released the team member to go and do his thing.

The collateral damage was a couple of dozen families. Some families were saved under my preaching, some were physically healed by my laying hands on them, and others received children after being declared barren. I could go on and on.

As David experienced with his men, when you lead, you will see ungrateful, arrogant, and childish behavior from people you believed in and served with your leadership.

Betrayal requires the proximity to kiss your cheek.

Jesus' entire ministry is marked by betrayal. Family members doubted him. Team members attempted to manipulate Him. His hometown rejected Him. The government was suspicious of Him. One of His disciples betrayed Him. The religious crowd crucified him.

But David found strength in the Lord his God. — 1 Samuel 30:6

As a leader, you must know how to strengthen yourself in the Lord.

Like David, strengthening yourself in the Lord requires a commitment to spiritual growth and a deepening relationship with God. Here are five key practices that can help you cultivate inner strength and resilience in the Lord:

1. **Seek God's Presence Regularly:** Dedicate daily time to

connect with God through prayer, meditation, and reading the Bible. Immerse yourself in His presence and allow His words to guide and strengthen your spirit.

2. **Develop a Deepened Understanding of God's Character:** Study the Bible and explore the attributes of God. Learn about His love, mercy, faithfulness, and power. You will develop a deeper trust and reliance on Him as you grasp His character. Sound doctrine and good theology are tied to knowing the character of God, not just learning about Him.

3. **Practice Gratitude and Praise:** Express gratitude for God's blessings in your life, both big and small. Praise Him for His goodness and faithfulness. Gratitude and praise shift your focus from problems to God's unwavering love, fostering inner peace and strength.

4. **Seek Fellowship with Other Believers:** Surround yourself with people who share your faith and values. Engage in fellowship, worship, and discussions about God's Word. The support and encouragement of fellow believers can be a powerful source of strength.

5. **Choose to Obey God's Will:** Make a conscious decision to align your actions with God's principles. Obey His commandments and seek His guidance in your daily decisions. Obedience demonstrates your trust in God and strengthens your spiritual foundation.

Remember, strengthening yourself in the Lord is a journey, not a destination. There will be ups and downs along the way. But by consistently practicing these keys, you can cultivate a deep and abiding faith that will empower you to face life's challenges with unwavering strength and resilience.

Then David said to Abiathar, the priest, the son of Ahimelek, "Bring me the ephod." Abiathar brought it to him, and David inquired of the Lord, "Shall I pursue this raiding party? Will I overtake them?"

"Pursue them," he answered. "You will certainly overtake them and succeed in the rescue." 1 Samuel 30:7-8

I love this!

After David encouraged himself in the Lord, he retrieved the ephod to inquire about God.

An ephod (Hebrew: דּוֹפֵא) was a type of ceremonial garment worn by priests in ancient Israel. It was a sleeveless vest or apron typically made of fine linen or wool. The ephod was usually decorated with gold embroidery and precious stones. It was also often adorned with two shoulder straps and a breastplate called the hoshen. The hoshen contained the Urim and Thummim, objects used to seek knowledge.

It was not restricted to be used only by the High Priest.

We do not need or use an ephod because you and I have access to the Holy Spirit.

The Holy Spirit plays a crucial role in the lives of Christians, providing guidance, comfort, and empowerment. In John 14 and 15, Jesus highlights five significant ways the Holy Spirit assists us in our spiritual journey:

1. **Teacher and Guide:** The Holy Spirit acts as our teacher, guiding us into all truth and reminding us of Jesus' teach-

ings. He helps us understand God's Word and discern His will for our lives. (John 14:26, 16:13)

2. **Comforter and Advocate:** The Holy Spirit serves as our comforter, providing solace and strength in times of distress and uncertainty. He offers reassurance and helps us navigate difficult situations with unwavering faith. (John 14:16, 16:7)

3. **Convictor and Empowerer:** The Holy Spirit convicts us of our sins and shortcomings, leading us to repentance and transformation. He also empowers us to live according to God's standards, enabling us to overcome temptations and pursue righteousness. (John 16:8, 15:26)

4. **Revealer and Witness:** The Holy Spirit reveals God's glory and majesty, deepening our understanding of His divine nature. He also serves as a witness to the truth about Jesus Christ and His saving grace. (John 15:26, 16:14)

5. **Intercessor and Helper:** The Holy Spirit intercedes on our behalf, bringing our prayers and petitions to the Father's throne. He acts as our helper, guiding us towards God's will and equipping us with the spiritual gifts needed to fulfill our calling. (Romans 8:26, 1 Corinthians 12:11)

The Holy Spirit's presence in our lives is a constant source of strength, guidance, and comfort. As we invite Him to dwell within us and yield to His influence, we experience a deepening relationship with God and the empowerment to live a life that honors Him.

With the guidance of the ephod, David rallied his men to action. They chased down the perpetrators and rescued all of the women and children, recovered their possessions, and acquired other goods and loot.

David did not surrender his leadership when facing challenges. He encouraged himself in the Lord, inquired from the Lord's instruction, and then engaged on the field of contest with his Champions.

Mentoring men.

According to a recent Barna data-driven guidebook, *Five Essentials to Engage Today's Men*, men's ministries should include — identity, vocation, well-being, relationships, and church engagement. This study closely aligns with what we've discovered in practice at FivestarMan — identity = purpose; vocation = entrepreneur; well-being = faithful; relationships = gallant; church engagement = philanthropic cause.

Here are the cold, hard facts:

- Only about 10% of congregations offer ongoing ministry programs for men (compared to about 90% of churches that provide women's and children's ministries).
- In churches that do offer men's ministry, **fewer than 20 percent** of the men actively participate. Most men in the congregation do not interact with the men's ministry.
- Men's ministry programs tend to be event-driven. Once the event is over, they quickly lose momentum. Hence, most men's ministry programs die out within two years of launch.
- Men's ministry typically does not disciple men.

Rather than examining every statistic and nuance of the study, let me just concur with their conclusion because, after thirteen years of dedicated efforts to minister to men, we have discovered some practicals and best practices to employ:

Message

> *Speak a message of wisdom among the mature, but not the wisdom of this age or of the rulers of this age, who are coming to nothing.* — *1 Corinthians 2:6*

The message of FivestarMan works because we do not speak down to men. Most efforts speak to men as if we were still boys. No, we speak a message among the mature.

Secondly, the message of FivestarMan works because we are not compromising our standards of Biblical/Authentic manhood. I've seen men's video curricula with guys sitting around drinking whiskey and smoking cigars, basking in their liberality, talking about being men. I don't believe that I must return to what I went to the altar to get over. I grew up as a heathen — alcohol, tobacco, and cussing were the norm. I'd rather have holiness, wholesome talk, health, and a sober-mind.

We speak directly to the purposes of a man's heart. Remember, we've defined them as:

1. Adventure
2. Entrepreneur
3. Gallant
4. Faithful
5. Philanthropic

When you focus on a man's purpose, his life becomes a passionate pursuit of authentic manhood. Proverbs says that understanding draws purposes out of the heart. Understanding is like the bucket reaching into the well of water so that we can drink from it.

Strategy

I asked the Holy Spirit to help me understand our strategy to reach men. After much prayer and fasting, He said, *"Look at Habakkuk 2:2."*

> ***"Write my answer plainly on tablets,***
> ***so that a runner can carry the correct message to others.***
> ***This vision is for a future time.***
> ***It describes the end, and it will be fulfilled.***
> ***If it seems slow in coming, wait patiently,***
> ***for it will surely take place.***
> ***It will not be delayed." —Habakkuk 2:2***

Although I have read this passage hundreds of times, I never saw it with the applicable revelation that I did at that time. I concluded that this passage is today's modern-day understanding of men's ministry.

1. **Write my answer plainly.** We must speak clearly to men without confusing language or water-down versions of masculinity. Men need to hear answers to today's challenges.
2. **Deliver the message on tablets.** In 2022, adults spent 5 hours daily on their phones. Mobile phones generated

over 70% of website traffic in 2022, with desktops only generating 30%. This led us to transform FivestarMan.com from an informational website to a personalized journey for Biblical/Authentic manhood.

3. **Men must be empowered to take the message and run with it.** We can't expect men in today's climate to become idle. Too many programs attempt to persuade men to sit and have 'quiet time.' Men need a message that they can run with. That's why we created TheDailyChampion.com to deliver a word of encouragement so that men can read, listen, or watch it as they go. Our goal is to transform their daily commute into a time of communion.

4. **They can carry the message to others.** The message must be so clear that men can communicate it to others without using obscure Christian language. Every man can relate to the five passions that we've defined. Giving them an understanding of their purposes will attract them to know Jesus Christ.

5. **The vision is for a future time.** We're in the future time of the vision. There has never been a better opportunity than now to reach men. The most extraordinary move of God among men will happen now.

6. **It describes the end, and it will be fulfilled.** We're certainly living in the last days. Now, more than ever, we need strong men to stand up and represent Christ in their homes, workplaces, churches, communities, and nations.

7. **If it seems slow in coming, wait patiently.** I have to admit these last thirteen years required tenacity. For the first few years, I constantly hit a wall of resistance. Some thought that I was harsh and mean-spirited. I may have been. I saw things coming that no one was paying attention to. They

were distracted by the trivial.

Social Media

The following statistics are alarming. However, we must use the platforms available to us. Rather than curse what is happening, we need to reshape and use these platforms to our advantage. We're constantly working to improve our reach on these platforms.

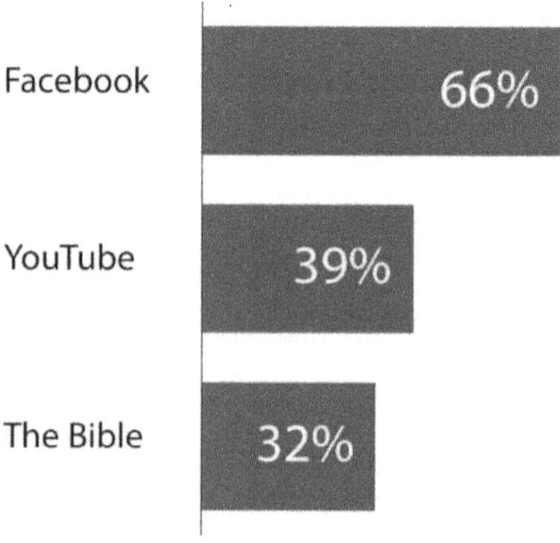

Notes: For social media use, the number equals the percentage of evangelical by belief respondents who when asked "About how often do you visit or use the following social media platforms?" selected "about once a day" or "several times a day."
For Bible use, the number equals the percentage of evangelical by belief respondents who when asked, "Not including as part of a church worship service, how often do you read the Bible?" selected "every day."
Source: LifeWay Research http://lifewayresearch.com/wp-content/uploads/2019/09/ERLC-Civility-Report.pdf

We must stop dismissing those who are connecting with our message online. They're not just watchers; they are connectors.

Reread Habakkuk 2:2; it is a remarkable insight into the opportunity that we have to reach men without the limitations of time and distance.

For example, when I wake up in the morning, grab my coffee, and go into my office/studio to read the Word of God, pray, and praise God, tens of thousands of men are reading TheDailyChampion.com with me. Our Executive Director of FivestarMan Brazil says that we're reaching over 100,000 men in Brazil with the message of Biblical/Authentic manhood.

Our goal is to continue to expand in the United States, Brazil, Chile, and around the world. We are working now with translations for every available language. With the tools of Artificial Intelligence (AI), this could have within months, not years.

The Rhythm of Mentoring Men

I've advised that we look at the calendar year of men's lives to determine best practices that will spiritually influence their lives.

1. **Encourage Daily:** Encourage one another every day, as long as it is called "today," that the deceitfulness of sin may harden none of you. (Hebrews 3:13) Men need a word of encouragement. Every day, we should pray about who we should reach out to speak an exhorting word to. You

will be amazed how God will use you in this. I ask the Holy Spirit to help me know who I could call and encourage. I am humored and humbled when they answer the phone and say, "Neil, that is so strange. I was just thinking about you when you called." It has happened so often that I know the Holy Spirit is using me in this opportunity. That is why I took the laborious work to write TheDailyChampion.com. I want men to be encouraged in a very troubling time in this world.

2. **Engage Weekly:** Men need a small strategic gathering of men to engage with. This is the strategy that Jesus employed to disciple men. It makes sense that we should copy his strategy. I don't segregate the ages of males. I believe that young men need to engage with seasoned men. I think that they share mutual benefits. The seasoned bring wisdom to the group. The young bring energy and excitement.

3. **Excursions Monthly:** Men relate on the field of contest. We love yard games — football, baseball, hockey, soccer, golf, hunting, et cetera. Men relate on the field. Our fellowship comes naturally outside playing games, doing projects, and adventuring.

4. **Encounters Quarterly:** Remember, God promised that men should corporately come together and worship. Then, they will have an encounter with Him. He would give us increase, protection, and promotion when we do. We've learned that a Friday night inspirational service with carefully crafted music designed for men and a strong empowering message is vital for men to have a mountain-top experience with God. We follow that up with a Breakfast of Champions to give practical instruction for men to transform their daily

commute into communion.

5. **Exploits Yearly:** Not only is man designed to gather revenue, but men are also designed to scatter resources to others. Expressing the philanthropic cause is what we call an exploit. We've seen some amazing things happen when men get turned to using their gifts to better mankind.

Every gathering of men needs a leader.

With our new website being a personalized journey to Biblical/Authentic manhood, we are also building **FivestarMan 300** so that men can be equipped to lead men.

Stepping up to leadership.

When Jesus wanted to launch his ministry and secure the Message of the Gospel, He carefully selected and engaged a few common men— primarily hard-working entrepreneurs. **Although outwardly ordinary, these men were also gifted.** Their time with Jesus empowered them to become used in extraordinary capacities (see Acts 4:13).

One of the obstacles early in my ministry was my ordinariness— I was not naturally gifted in ministry—meaning my gift set did not lend to being useful, much less to be successful in ministry. However, my obvious weakness exposed a strength.

I discovered that I have an ability to discern the gifts within others.

Let me be very transparent with you. At times, as leaders, we are reticent to hand off the work of ministry for a variety of reasons that may have a measure of justification. I've recruited, trained, and released men to do the work only to face disappointment and the regret of failed work or dishonest gain.

My discernment of a person's gift often overshadowed the

flaws within their character. After repeatedly experiencing the disappointment of failed leaders, I considered withdrawing from trusting anyone with the work of ministry. However, here's what I've learned as a pastor:

> **My enemy doesn't have to deceive me; he just has to distract me.**

One of our enemy's most successful schemes is **keeping us busy at the expense of doing what is effective.**

Activity doesn't always mean productivity.
Jesus spent approximately three years in his earthly ministry, trained men to do the work, and then left them with it. He placed a huge amount of trust in those men to do the work of ministry. Just as Jesus recruited and released men, we should also discern those who are gifted, prove their character, and empower them to lead.

Here's what you can expect to see happen in the men of your church:

- He will become more **outgoing** and **adventurous**. He will become a **leader** in his **life**, **marriage**, **work**, and **church**. He will begin to condition himself and create new **energy** and **excitement** for **life** and **God**.
- He may **start a new business**, and discovering his **entrepreneurial drive** will motivate him **to be productive**. He will become more aware of his **abilities** and **financial success**.

- Your men will **turn their hearts to their wives and children**. They will become **gallant**—and **honorable** toward women by reigniting their relationships. They will avoid the pitfalls of inappropriate relationships and the trappings of the sexual culture.
- Men will become more **faithful—honest, authentic, and spiritual**. Their walk with God will become a daily commute. They will habitually read the Word of God with a new sense of intrigue and enthusiasm.
- They will also develop a long-term view of life, desiring to leave a legacy. **They will become men of great exploits.**

Agreement versus accountability.

The Achilles heel of men's ministries is the notion that states, "We must hold each other accountable."

> **That does not mean we want to dominate you by telling you how to put your faith into practice. We want to work together with you so you will be full of joy, for it is by your own faith that you stand firm. — 2 Corinthians 1:24**

Paul says, *"My job is not to dominate you but by working together."* How can two walk toward a destination unless we agree on the direction?

Think of the benefits of a coach.

A coach is an instructor of gifts. He draws on the potential of a person to excel in their endeavor. They are using training and discipline to attract the best out of a man.

> *Iron sharpens iron,*
>> *So one man sharpens another.* — **Proverbs** 27:17

Iron sharpens by the clash, not by the caress. We must have someone in our lives that sharpens us. They intend to make us better, not embittered.

> **A man gains wisdom either through a mentor or through pain.**

In the above scripture, 2 Corinthians 1:24, the Apostle Paul reveals that each man will only stand firm by the practice of his own faith.

> **God gave man dominion over the earth, not domination over other men.**

Domination: *The exercise of control or influence over someone or something, or the state of being so controlled; submitted to the rule of another.*

We have been taught the issue with men is we're not accountable. If we enter into male-to-male relationships, we position ourselves to live the disciplined life of holiness by submission. This theory subscribes to the notion that "shame" is a great motivator.

Here are some obvious problems with this philosophy of men's ministry:

- Accountability positions men's leaders as judges. A man must live the righteousness of other men.

- Accountability positions the "submitted" as a child or woman. It causes a grown man to be spoken down to.
- In attempting to implement this accountability strategy, many men's ministries have adopted militaristic themes and protocols as a strategy.
- When men are forced into this perversion of the peer-to-peer relationship, authentic manhood is weakened, emasculated, and effeminate.
- Every man who has ever asked me to hold him accountable eventually stopped talking to me.
- The suggestion is that we need men to open their hearts and release their emotions to purify themselves.

Men are emotional; however, the emotions of men are directly related to their purposes. His purposes reside in his heart.

The word **heart** means "seat of purposes; seat of appetites; seat of emotions." The residence of purposes is within the heart of a man. When he understands his purposes, he dictates the appetites that determine his emotions. Paul said, *"We want to work together so that you will be full of joy."*

> **If a man lives by emotions, he has an uncontrolled appetite and perverts his purpose.**

When I speak to the five purposes of authentic manhood, I've found that men commit themselves to living them out and become very passionate about pursuing them.

How do we lead men? By taking on the nature of a coach, speaking an encouraging word—someone who knows how to draw upon the gifts within a man and sharpen his life skills.

- A good coach doesn't clone players to be as good as he was — he challenges players to be as good as they can be.
- Encourage one another daily, as long as it is called **Today**, so that sin's deceitfulness may harden none of you. Hebrews 3:13
- A coach edifies, encourages, corrects, and sometimes rebukes; however, the motivation is to calibrate a man to the standard of God's original intent of authentic manhood and his purpose.

This may seem a bit nit-picky on this subject, but in reality— using the accountability philosophy for men's ministries has been a repellent for reaching men.

Influencing Men

> *You yourself must be an example to them by doing good works of every kind. Let everything you do reflect the integrity and seriousness of your teaching. — Titus 2:7*

John Maxwell defined leadership as influence. The simplicity of this statement captures a very complex debate on what it means to be a leader.

> **Leadership is influencing and empowering others to change and making intelligent choices to advance their cause.**

Leadership draws upon the potential of those with whom they are influencing.

Paul told Timothy to be a man worthy of imitation. The example in what you say, in the way you live, in your love, your faith, and your purity is to make a mark, an impression upon others. (Read 1 Timothy 4:12)

Please understand—we're seasoned and serious men involved in good work. We're not playing games! There is a level of maturity that we must bring to the table. You can't be seen as the jester if you want to be a leader of men.

This does not mean that you won't have fun; we need to take this business of speaking to men seriously.

- Integrity commands influence.
- Men become a moral force and emanate spiritual influence.
- A FivestarMan will gain the power to change or affect someone.
- As a leader of men, your example will empower others, but you will find that leading men comes with spiritual empowerment.
- Most of us can describe a man who affected our lives, even if they were unaware of their direct influence.
- Your words will become weighty, measured, and intentional. You will be prompted by the Holy Spirit on what to say and, equally importantly—what **not** to say.

Everyone enjoys a fitting reply; it is wonderful to say the right thing at the right time! -Proverbs 15:23

With the position of authority, we must be sober-minded and not flippant with our influence. Even Jesus submitted his words to the direction intent of His Father.

The words I speak are not my own, but my Father who lives in me does his work through me. -John 14:10

Jesus didn't wing it (so to speak). He was very intentional when talking to men.

As we deliver the content (curriculum for Engage and messages for Encounters), you will see there is intentional direction in where we are going. We rely heavily upon the Holy Spirit to guide us on what and how to say it. That doesn't mean that we're infallible; just simply working diligently to *"speak clearly as we should, making the most of every opportunity and that our conversation is seasoned with salt."* (Colossians 4:6)

One of the fundamental challenges we've seen in ministries to men is using the unintentional approach to leading men. You see this when small groups are unprepared, men's events do not have a cohesive message, and leaders lack thoughtful preparation.

To attract men to the table of Biblical/Authentic manhood and to keep them engaged, we must honor their time by being seasoned, serious in our approach, and confident that what we are speaking has directional intent. Doing so will help them make intelligent choices.

The Qualities of a Capable Man of Leadership

By now, I'm sure you're ready to reach men and see families change.

"What you have heard from me in the presence of many witnesses entrust to faithful men who will be able to teach others also." -2 Timothy 2:2

"Select from all the people some capable, honest men who fear God and hate bribes. Appoint them as leaders over groups. " - *Exodus 18:21*

"Select seven men who are well respected and are full of the Spirit and wisdom." - *Acts 6:2*

The Qualities of a Capable Man are listed as follows:

1. **CAPABLE:** Ability to show oneself strong, to display courage, ability, and efficiency.
2. **HONEST:** Stable, integrity, firm, and true to form.
3. **FEAR GOD:** Inspired reverence, honor, and awe for God, the Church, and respect toward Believers.
4. **HATE BRIBES:** One who hates gain by unrighteous means, opposed to unethical influence, doesn't profit from the position.
5. **WELL RESPECTED:** A good report; reputation; affirmed that one has seen, heard, or experienced something.
6. **FULL OF THE SPIRIT:** Spirit-empowered; Spirit-led; a man with no vacuum, space, or margin of fleshly desires.
7. **WISDOM:** Skill in management of affairs; experienced, discerning, contemplative; the ability to forecast the outcome of decisions.

You will keenly discern in selecting men to do the work. As you see men interacting with one another, you will notice the Influencers. They're not sophomoric—always jesting and jarring with others. They're not novices—these men have some experiences in life. They could very well be young, but they still have a season to them.

Now, let's turn ordinary men into Champions.

10

Mighty Men & Great Exploits

"These are the names of David's mighty warriors." — 2 Samuel 23:1

David has just spoken his last words. His words are weighty. They are inspired utterances. He is the exalted man of God. A warrior. A musician. A leader of men.

David says, "The Spirit of the Lord spoke through me; his word was on my tongue."

As a leader, if the Spirit can ever use us to speak His words to encourage men, we will have done well.

> *When one rules over people in righteousness,*
>   *when he rules in the fear of God,*
>   *he is like the light of morning at sunrise*
>   *on a cloudless morning,*
>   *like the brightness after rain*
>   *that brings grass from the earth.' — 2 Samuel 23:3-4*

I want to stress the magnitude of leading men.

Again, after spending the last thirteen years speaking to men across the country and in other nations, I have seen that our efforts to reach men are minuscule and treated as unnecessary.

David proves that by leading men, we change our destinies.

Mighty Men of David

The Three

Josheb-Basshebeth

His name means recliner. He is the original Lazy Boy. He is known for being a dweller in rest. Yet, David spoke words to Josh and drew out of him a Champion. He became an elite soldier. He was the leader of the Three (an exceptional unit in David's forces).

Josh stood against eight hundred men and killed them all in one encounter!

Eleazar

He was one of the elite Three. He stood with David in a battle against the Philistines at Pas Dammim. The Israelites retreated, but Eleazar stood his ground and fought until his hand grew tired and froze to the sword. When the Israelite army returned, they could only strip the dead because the battle was over.

Shammah

When the Philistines banded together at the field of lentils, again, the Israelites fled, but Shammah stood in the middle of the field and fought. Shammah won the victory and protected the harvest field.

One time, while David was in the stronghold, the Cave of Adullam, he breathed a sigh of longing for the spring water from the well near the gate of Bethlehem.

The elite Three risked their lives, broke through the enemy lines, drew water from the well, and carried it back to David.

Can you imagine that kind of dedication?

David refused to drink it. Instead, he worshiped God. Turned the spring water into an offering and poured it on the ground.

Benaiah

He was a brave warrior. He did great exploits. He struck down two of the champions of Moab. He chased a lion into a pit on a snowy day and killed it. He also struck down an Egyptian giant. The Egyptian had a spear, while Benaiah only had a club. Ben snatched the spear from the Egyptian and killed him with it.

He was not one of the Three, but he was as famous.

30 Mighty Men

I want to list the thirty mighty men and what their names mean. Names can be descriptive of a man's personality. Names can be prophetic. In the Jewish mind, a name is a book. So, you can know a lot about a person by knowing their name.

- Asahel: God-made.
- Elhanan: God has been gracious.
- Shammah the Harodite: Astonishment.
- Elika: My God opposes.
- Helez: He has saved.
- Ira: Overseer and protector of a city.
- Abiezer: My Father is helping.
- Mebunnai: Temple of Jehovah.
- Zalmon: One who covers, protects.
- Maharai: One who acts without hesitation.

- Heleb: Milk or fat. Also means anointed.
- Ittai: With me, brotherhood.
- Benaiah (Pirathonite): Jehovah has built.
- Hiddai: Rejoicing in Jehovah.
- Abialbon: God is my father.
- Azmaveth: Strong unto death.
- Eliahba: Whom God hides.
- Shammah, the Hararite: Astonishment.
- Ahiam: named after his uncle.
- Eliphelet: God is deliverance.
- Eliam: God is kinsman.
- Hezro: Enclosed.
- Paarai: Expanding, wide-open.
- Igal: He redeems.
- Bani: Built like a man.
- Zelek, the Ammonite: Split.
- Naharai: literally, snorter. Figuratively, a man of extremes.
- Ira: Overseer and protector of a city.
- Gareb: Scabby, one covered with marks on the skin.
- Uriah: Jehovah is my light.

***The Spirit came upon Amasai, the leader of the Thirty,
and he said,***

> ***"We are yours, David!***
> ***We are on your side, son of Jesse.***
> ***Peace and prosperity be with you,***
> ***and success to all who help you,***
> ***for your God is the one who helps you." 1 Chronicles
12:18***

There were hundreds of mighty men. All of them were expert archers, and they could shoot arrows or sling stones with their left hand as well as their right.

Some brave and experienced warriors from the tribe of Gad also defected to David while he was at the stronghold in the wilderness. They were expert with both shield and spear, as fierce as lions and as swift as deer on the mountains.

The weakest among them could take on a hundred regular troops, and the strongest could take on a thousand!

Day after day, more men joined David until he had a great army, like the army of God.

David's army became thousands of brave men.

Here are five qualities of a mighty man who does great exploits according to the Bible:

1. **Courage:** A mighty man is not afraid of challenges or adversity. He faces them head-on with bravery and determination. For example, despite his small stature, David fearlessly confronted Goliath, a giant warrior who instilled fear in the hearts of many. (1 Samuel 17:45-51)
2. **Faith:** A mighty man has unwavering faith in God. He believes God is always with him and will guide him through any situation. David's faith in God gave him the strength to defeat Goliath, knowing God would be with him in battle. (1 Samuel 17:47)
3. **Strength:** A mighty man is physically and mentally strong. He can endure hardships and overcome obstacles. Samson, known for his extraordinary physical strength, used his power to fight against the Philistines, Israel's enemies. (Judges 13-16)

4. **Wisdom:** A mighty man possesses wisdom and discernment. He makes wise decisions and acts with sound judgment. Renowned for his wisdom, Solomon made fair and just rulings, leading to peace and prosperity in Israel during his reign. (1 Kings 3:5-12)

5. **Humility:** A mighty man is humble and does not seek recognition for his accomplishments. He gives credit to God and acknowledges his limitations. Joshua, a leader who led the Israelites into the Promised Land, attributed his successes to God's guidance and the strength of the people. (Joshua 4:14, 24)

These five qualities – courage, faith, strength, wisdom, and humility – are essential for anyone who aspires to do great exploits in the world. By embodying these traits, individuals can overcome challenges, inspire others, and positively impact the world around them.

What can God do through you?

I've seen so many men come to Christ, be empowered by the Holy Spirit, and gain an understanding of their purposes.

Each week, when we have our FivestarMan Champions Livestream, I see names of men dedicated to Biblical/Authentic manhood. I see men faithfully reading TheDailyChampion.com each day. I meet men coming to weekend encounters and our AUTHENTIC FivestarMan conferences. I am humbled by what God is doing in the lives of men today.

Yet, there is so much more that God wants to do in our time and through men like you.

Yes, I am calling you out.

I believe there is more in you than what you've achieved.

I think of a young man who dreamed of owning his own business, yet he was stuck in the routine of being a wage slave. He read one of my books, Seven Laws Which Govern Increase and Order, and became inspired to take the risk and start his company. From seven customers, he now has over seven hundred customers who pay him a monthly residual for his services. He is consistently one of our most faithful partners.

I think of a man who made a career change after pastoring for twenty-five years; he felt called to expand into the financial business. He is now managing over $100 million in assets.

I think of authors and artists who were inspired to write and sing, reaching millions. I was presented with a Gold Record from one group that I mentored.

I think of a private pilot who was a glorified air chauffeur for his boss. But he got inspired by one of my messages, stepped out to start his own company, and now has one of the largest private jet fleets in the nation.

I think of the man who destroyed his life by compromising with pornography but read the book *Bedding Ishtar*, repented, and committed his life to purity of purpose. He has seen God restore his marriage.

I think of the Appalachian pastor who dreamed of building a new church on a beautiful piece of property, yet all his leaders told him it couldn't be done. He read my book, Seven Laws Which Govern Increase and Order, and three years later, he asked me to dedicate his building packed with people. I recently was able to celebrate his fifteenth year in that building!

I think of the Mighty Man of God who leads thousands of technical engineers in San Diego. Yet, he has a dream of leading men to Christ. He read my book, Centurion Principle, and began to teach men in small groups. He is now part of the lead team at a mega-church leading men!

I think of another middle-aged man who has launched two companies on the path to selling one of his companies for $50 to $100 million.

I think of the Associate Pastor who has long had a passion for men's ministries but did not have the messaging and strategy to make it happen. Then, suddenly, he discovered the resources that we offer. Now, he leads men and makes a massive difference in his church.

I think of the young man attending a university who passion-ately pursues Biblical/Authentic manhood, putting aside what most men his age crave and chasing to position himself to reach men worldwide.

I think of the oil company owner who hired me and commis-sioned me to sit in on a few company meetings to simply discern what he needed to position his company to be purchased. This kind of mentoring, though unusual, saved him millions of dollars because he relied on the Holy Spirit to give him insight.

I could tell you about marriages restored, men healed of father wounds, families reunited, men getting off the couch and returning to work. I could talk about men resurrecting their health by reconditioning their bodies.

I think of the churches that we've partnered with mega-churches, small rural churches, and cowboy churches, yet all of them are seeing men's lives changed!

I encouraged a rural pastor that I encourage to reach men. I challenged him that if he worked the FivestarMan strategy, he would see at least ten men come to his church within a year. He took me up on the challenge and saw twenty-seven men and their families start attending his church.

I can point to the thousands who have accepted Jesus as their Savior and the men who have been Spiritually empowered.

Now is the time for you to step up to leadership. It is time for you to move from passivity to purpose.

I may not be a prophet, but I believe I am prophesying to you, **"It is time to leave the cave. Get back to the field of the contest and fulfill your purpose."**

I am here to encourage you! That's my purpose. That's our mission at FivestarMan!